CREEM

187 SOUTH WOODWARD AVENUE, SUITE 203, BIRMINGHAM, MICH. 48011
(313) 642-8833

Dear Jeffrey:

You always write us witty letters
even if we don't always print 'em;
so why don't you try your hand at
some record reviews (3-500 words)
or especially (for starters) some
Rockaramas, which can be anything
from a single word to a short
paragraph.

Best regards,

Lester Bangs

Lester Bangs

P.S- Also up for movie,
book reviews, & Beat Goes
Ons.

LESTER BANGS

Published 2021
New Haven Publishing
www.newhavenpublishingltd.com   newhavenpublishing@gmail.com

Cover Design by Jeffrey Morgan. Interior Design by Pete Cunliffe

newhaven
publishing

Copyright © 2021 Jeffrey Morgan
All rights reserved
ISBN: 978-1-912587-53-7

ROCK CRITIC CONFIDENTIAL
Written and Photographed by Jeffrey Morgan
Designed by Pete Cunliffe

TERMS AND CONDITIONS

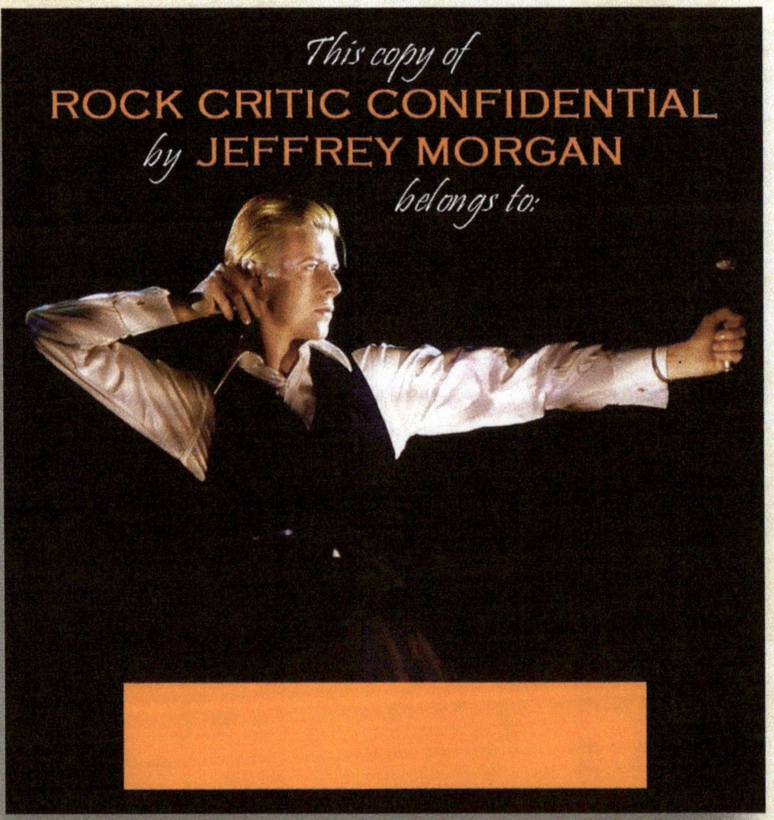
This copy of
ROCK CRITIC CONFIDENTIAL
by JEFFREY MORGAN
belongs to:

These are the rules. Terms and conditions may apply. Read carefully before proceeding. This product is intended for educational purposes only. Void where prohibited by law. Subject to availability. License No. 52746. For best results, use only as directed. List each item separately. Use extra page if necessary. Contents may settle during shipment. No other warranty expressed or implied. Check your local listings. Close cover before striking. Factory sealed for your protection. The black bands at the top and bottom of the picture are normal. Proof of purchase required. Do not use while operating a motor vehicle or heavy equipment. Postage will be paid by addressee. Please allow six to eight weeks for delivery. This is not an offer to sell securities. Past performance is no guarantee of future results. Read the prospectus thoroughly first. Does not represent an average user. Your results may vary. Visitors sign in with Security. Apply only to affected area. Handicapped parking only. May be too intense for some viewers. Confidential when completed. Thank you for calling. All of our operators are busy at the moment. Your call is important to us. Please stay on the line and a customer representative will be with you shortly. Calls may be monitored for quality control purposes. Do not stamp. Continued on other side. For recreational use only. Exact change only. Mind the gap. Keep arms and head in. Do not disturb. Last gas for 500 miles. Standing room only. All models are over 18 years of age. If symptoms persist consult your physician. Open other end. Electrical hazard. Risk of electric shock. No user-serviceable parts inside. If alarm sounds return to cashier. Best if used before due date. Subject to change without notice. All times approximate. Soon to be a major motion picture. Closed for the holidays. Seating is for customers only. Caution liquid is hot. Preheat oven to 450 and place on cookie sheet on middle rack. No parking. Everything must go. Final week. Unauthorized vehicles will be towed away at owner's expense. Simulated picture. May complicate pregnancy. Please remain seated until the ride has come to a complete stop. Breaking seal constitutes acceptance of agreement. For off-road use only. Maid please make up room. As seen on TV. May cause drowsiness do not drive or operate heavy machinery. For external use only. To open, push down, then turn. Repeat broadcast, do not call. Fasten seatbelt. One size fits all. Aim away from face. Trespassers will be prosecuted. Penalty for misuse: fine or imprisonment. Although inspired by actual events, this story is entirely fictional. This end up. Colors may fade. We have sent the forms which seem right for you. Slippery when wet. For office use only. Not affiliated with any organization. Postage Paid if mailed in the United States. Drop in any mailbox. Edited for television. Keep cool and process promptly. Not a through street. No shirt, no shoes, no service. Right lane must turn right. Post Office will not deliver without postage. The Surgeon General advises that danger to health increases with amount smoked. Never siphon by mouth. List was current at time of printing. Any use of this product other than the one for which it is intended is illegal. Return to sender. Must be of legal drinking age to enter. No radio inside. Not responsible for direct, indirect, incidental or consequential damages resulting from any defect, error or failure to perform. At participating locations only. Not the real thing but an incredible simulation. No disc inside. Please turn off all pagers and cellular phones before entering the theater. Unauthorized use is prohibited. No bills larger that $20. Keep off the grass. Late patrons will not be seated until first available break in the program. See label for sequence. It is a criminal offense to make false or misleading statements. Substantial penalty for early withdrawal. Price excludes license, insurance, applicable taxes, freight and PDE. Pay your server. Do not write below this line. Contains new material. Do not remove under penalty of law. Lost ticket pays maximum rate. Insert tab A into slot B. Free delivery with minimum $50 order. To order, contact your local cable company. Your canceled check is your receipt. Elevators are available for passengers with difficulty negotiating stairs. Place stamp here. This is not an exit. Do not feed the animals. May contain traces of peanut products. Paper jam, call key operator. Avoid contact with skin. Sanitized for your protection. Thank you for holding. Someone will be with you shortly. Be sure each item is properly endorsed. Sign here. Filmed before a live studio audience. Portions of this broadcast were prerecorded. Take this medication with food. Prices slightly higher in the east. Prices may vary in Hawaii, Alaska and Puerto Rico. Employees and their families are not eligible. Now a major motion picture. Store in a cool, dry place. Suggested serving. Not exactly as illustrated. Turn off engine. Not actual size. Enlarged to show texture. Add toner. Proceed with caution. Sound horn. In case of fire, break glass. Do not refreeze if thawed. Cook from frozen. Contestants have been briefed on some questions before the show. A promotional consideration was paid in return for this announcement. Limited time offer. Call now to ensure prompt delivery. Use of this card acknowledges receipt of and agreement by the cardholder to the terms of any agreement(s) which from time to time govern any banking services for which the card may be used. You may already be a winner. In the event of an emergency, proceed in an orderly fashion to the nearest exit. Walk, do not run. Return for refund in MI, KY, VT, OR, MD and NY. You must be present to win. No passes accepted for this engagement. Buyer beware. Check purchase before leaving. Not transferable. Payable in U.S. funds only. Due to illness the starring roll in this afternoon's performance will be played by the understudy. Women's model only. Other products and companies referred to herein are trademarks or registered trademarks of their respective companies or mark holders. No purchase necessary. Buy one, get one free. Do not incinerate. Ticket holders line up here. Refrigerate after opening. Unsolicited submissions will not be accepted. The following is a test of the Emergency Broadcast System. Take a number for faster service. Processed at location stamped in code at top of carton. Shading within a garment may occur. Use only in a well-ventilated area. Keep in a dry place away from spark or open flame. Contents may explode under pressure. Deposit required. Replace with same type. Approved for veterans. Wristband policy is in effect. Stay tuned to this station for more details. Some equipment shown is optional. Price does not include taxes. American funds accepted at par. Not recommended for children. Prerecorded for this time zone. Mail back unused portion of product for complete refund of price of purchase. No cameras or recording devices allowed. No solicitors. Restaurant package not for resale. Do not send cash in mail. Photocopies and facsimiles are not accepted. For a full set of contest rules, send self-addressed stamped envelope to the above address. Check here if tax deductible. Do not open. Recommended for calorie-reduced diets. All other uses constitute fraud. Choking hazard: not for children under the age of six. All entries submitted become our property. Member FDIC. Based on double occupancy for 7 days/6 nights. Letters may be edited for length or clarity. List at least two alternate selections. A 20% gratuity has been added. Accessories extra. You have the right to remain silent. Anything you say can and will be used against you in a court of law. You have the right to an attorney. If you cannot afford an attorney, one will be provided for you. This film is not yet rated. The following preview has been approved for all audiences. First pull up, then pull down. Do not dry clean. For further information call the toll free number on your screen. Driver does not carry cash. Some of the trademarks mentioned in this product appear for identification purposes only. Place all metal objects in tray before proceeding through security. Not legal tender. Not legal for trade. Objects in mirror may be closer than they appear. Management reserves the right to refuse admittance. This broadcast is intended solely for the private use of our audience. Any recording, retransmission or rebroadcast of this program either in whole or in part without the express written consent of Major League Baseball is strictly prohibited. Do not leave child unattended. For the purposes of the Berne Convention, this teleplay is the work of this network and/or its affiliated stations. Record additional transactions on back of previous stub. Do not touch. No animals were harmed during the making of this picture. Harmful or fatal if swallowed. Do not fold, crush, bend, spindle or mutilate. This film not to be copied. Silence please. On approved credit. Credits are not contractual. Do not start engine until vessel has docked. Please move to the back of the bus. Coming soon to a theater near you. Good only on day issued. Do not drop. Keep engine running, put gearshift in neutral. Unsafe at any speed. Maximum capacity: 15 people or 3000 lbs. Do not puncture. Estimated street price. Wait until coins completely drop in slot before opening door. No refund or exchange. All sales final. Ship's registry: Liberia/Norway. Fragile handle with care. Those who appreciate quality enjoy it responsibly. Use in moderation. Not available in PA or NJ, not licensed in NY. Images were single-pass scanned at 300 dpi. Package sold by weight, not volume. Your mileage may vary. Not for use with some sets. Adult situations. Kids, get your parents' permission first before you call. This is an independent expenditure not approved by any candidate nor is any candidate responsible for it. I approved this message. Do not remove tag. Operators are standing by to take your call. No ticket no laundry. Professional driver on closed course. Don't try this at home. Cut on dotted line. Do not write in this space. Contact your branch. Screen images are simulated. Use as a motor fuel only. Not available in all colors. Includes the hit single. You are under no obligation to buy. Washrooms are for customer use only. Loading and unloading of passengers only. Employee does not have combination to safe. Limit one item per family. License, title, taxes, shipping, dealer prep not included in base sticker price. No rain checks. One way only. No smoking. 10 Eastern, 7 Pacific, 6 Mountain. Watch your step. No substitutions. Professional models not intended to represent actual people. Retain your stub. Safe operates on a time lock. Detach here. Keep out of reach of children. Don't drink and drive. The following program contains material that may be offensive to some viewers. Viewer discretion is advised. We are temporarily experiencing some difficulties. Please stand by. No cash on premises. Viewers strongly cautioned. Children under 18 not admitted without a parent or guardian. For renewals or change of address, please include current mailing label. Second Class Postage paid at St. Louis, MO. You must be this tall to ride. Minimum system requirements: current OS. 404 Error: The page you are seeking cannot be found at this location. Police line do not cross. Offer good only in the U.S. Operator does not provide change. Park and lock it. Not responsible for lost or missing items. Do not use if seal is broken. Persons with a heart condition, nursing mothers or others with a medical condition should seek the advice of a physician. Lather, rinse, repeat. Maximum headroom 12'5". Do not exceed maximum dosage of eight tablets in 12 hours. No waiting. Keep hands clear. Remember to take packages and belongings with you. See booklet for track listing. Remain behind white line and do not talk to the operator while vehicle is in motion. Do not dispose of used batteries in fire. Sign on the dotted line. There is enough mediation in this package to seriously harm a child. The number you have reached is out of service. Please hang up and try your call again. This is a recording. Please hang up now. Celebrity endorsement not implied. Admittance restricted to 18 years of age or older. Hearing protectors must be worn. Do not attempt. No unauthorized persons beyond this point. Access all areas. No step. May not be compatible with previous versions. Check requirements first. The picture has been modified from its original version and formatted to fit your screen. No food or drink allowed inside. Lyrics used by permission. Not valid in Alaska, Hawaii, Puerto Rico or other FPO. Send check or money order to the address on your screen. Sorry, no CODs. Use as required. You cannot be turned down. No salesman will call. Unauthorized duplication is a violation of applicable laws. Put tray in upright position. You break it, you bought it. Flush with water. Do not induce vomiting. Consult physician immediately. Not exactly as illustrated. Any resemblance to real persons, living or dead, is purely coincidental. Dealer may sell for less. Subject to approval. Some assembly required. Batteries not included. Read the fine print before signing. Accept no imitations. Marcas Registradas. Pat. Pending. Ignorance of the law is no excuse. Tell it to the judge. The moral right of the author has been asserted. Copyright © ® 2021 Jeffrey Morgan™. All rights reserved. You know the rules. The end.

DEDICATION

†

Jeffrey Morgan dedicates his life to Jesus Christ (Romans 6:23);
his life's work to the glory of God (1 Corinthians 10:31);
and he thanks the Holy Spirit for keeping him
on the narrow path (Matthew 7:13-14).

†

Photographed by Jeffrey Morgan

MYTH-MAKING OR MIRTH-MAKING?

by Robert Matheu

I sometimes confuse them. But not this time because this opening ramble is to officially state for posterity that *Rock Critic Confidential* **is both myth-making and mirth-making at its finest** *and* **funniest. Compromising photographs. Third degree interrogations. If there's a safe space for rock stars... This isn't it.**

As I've stated many times about my own work, I didn't always have a preconceived concept, the best were collaborations. And Jeffrey Morgan and I have been the very best of collaborators ever since I invited him to write for the original CREEM website in 2003. It's easy to miss the entire point of what Jeffrey and I have done since then. It should be the main power point, with a pointed emphasis on the powerful. As I once told Jeffrey: We were all a part of the same ride: you, me, Lou, Ted, Pop, we were on the same journey. We all knew we had the same thing in common, that's why we got the respect and the distain. For the both of us, however, the rewards weren't gold records on the wall, it was sharing the passion for the music that defined our life.

☆☆☆

Both *Rock Critic Confidential* (writing-based with accompanying photographs) and my own *The Perfect View* (photography-based with accompanying writing) are twin autobiographical companion pieces which not only share that passion, but literally define our entire lives. Two inverted yet complimentary volumes that, combined, are a written and photographic history of rock's greatest rollers. Best read as they were assembled: random, unfolding, organically.

Morganically, now more than ever,

Jeffrey *is* rock 'n' roll's most entertaining writer. Nobody else even come close. His writing is always true to the old CREEM style because Jeffrey's *natural* style is the old CREEM style. Always has and always will be. That's what Lester saw in Jeffrey's letters to the editor: that he writes in that style *all the time*. Jeffrey never stops. That's a good thing. Which is why *Rock Critic Confidential* is *the* benchmark primer on how to write with some *vitality* to it, instead of the dry-as-dust rust that *everyone* else hacks out these days.

There have been previous collections of rock writing, but this is the world's first anthology of rock criticism to see print as a profusely illustrated hardcover coffee table book. That's because, unlike all the others, Jeffrey is both a world-class rock critic *and* a world-class rock photographer. It's no coincidence that he began both careers almost simultaneously in 1974, first by interviewing KISS on September 14th and then by photographing Rick Wakeman on October 7th. It's also no coincidence that *Rock Critic Confidential* has the same classic lo-fi look and feel of a '70s large format rock read.

☆☆☆

As for Jeffrey's photographs, they speak for themselves. Or, as I remarked after he once showed me some of them for review: "What do you need *me* for?" Others are content to photograph musicians performing. Jeffrey photographs them *pausing*. That's why his concept of capturing the visual space *between* the musical notes is so inspired. It results in portraits that go beyond the usual forced, desperate, disconnected, and uninteresting photos whose hallmarks are style over substance and all digital manipulation. Not everyone can do it. Several times I've sat in a front row center seat next to a writer friend who had a camera in his hand, but none of them ever took anything worth seeing twice. When they say that you've got to have *the eye*, it's not just a saying, it's the truth. Jeffrey has it.

☆☆☆

I love being a part of this book and I love that Jeffrey counted our collaboration on the Keith Richards and Johnny Depp piece as worthy for inclusion. And yes, that story he tells at the beginning about how they both got a laugh out of it is indeed true—especially the part about "Deppo"

bringing it up to me in conversation ten years later when I ran into him one sunny Hollywood afternoon. He really did remember it.

Ahhh yes, it's all coming back to me now. I have more to say about the definitive in-depth interviews and the spot-on television parodies, but before I continue, I'll need my friend and editor Jeffrey to look over what I've already written a couple of times because his scrutiny is always appreciated, not to mention his encouragement over the years. I once sent him for editing some Stooges liner notes I wrote and Jeffrey sent them back to me untouched saying: "What do you need *me* for?" No wonder we get on so well.

☆☆☆

Now go and enjoy the wit and wisdom of Jeffrey Morgan's *Rock Critic Confidential*. I did. Best laugh before coffee I've had in some time.

ROBERT MATHEU

The photography of ROBERT MATHEU *has appeared on over 200 album covers and 500 magazine covers worldwide in addition to having been printed in such prestigious publications as:* Playboy, Vogue, Rolling Stone, Life, Time, Harpers, Mojo, Melody Maker, New York Times, Los Angeles Times, Hootch, *and* CREEM *to name only a dozen. His books include the HarperCollins hardcover anthology* CREEM: America's Only Rock 'n' Roll Magazine *and the Abrams hardcover history* The Stooges: The Authorized And Illustrated Story.

In 2018, Robert Matheu died suddenly before he could complete photo editing Rock Critic Confidential *and finish assembling his own first career-spanning edition of photographs,* The Perfect View. *He is sorely missed.*

A FOREWORD AND A WARNING

by Machine Rock

Telling the truth can be dangerous business. Honest and popular don't go hand in hand.
— Lyle Rogers and Chuck Clarke, "Dangerous Business"

Jeffrey Morgan has been blessed with many bouquets of affectionate appellations over the course of his long illustrious Truth-seekin' Truth-speakin' career, but without a doubt the single most offensively slanderous slur he ever had slung in his direction was when Cars keyboardist Greg Hawkes actually had the audacity to ask him: "Are you a musicologist?" Hawkes may have deemed it an innocuous enough enquiry, but from the way Morgan recoiled you'd have thought that he'd been called a journalist. "Get thee behind me!" he sternly rebuked. "I'm a rock critic!" Selah!

After all, you don't get to be a rock critic by sitting around with a buncha egghead musicians and having intimate little tête-à-têtes about the arcane minutiae of some obscure backwater record label that no one's ever heard of. And you *certainly* don't receive threatening letters from such cry-babies as Who guitarist Pete Townshend and Pink Floyd producer Bob Ezrin; or have a sob-sister like Amboy Dukes guitarist Ted Nugent haul off and slug you in the shoulder—as has happened to Morgan—by going to some highfalutin hoity-toity journalism school that's ill-equipped to prepare you for what to do when Lou "Shoot The Messenger" Gramm of Foreigner comes after you, irrationally irate over an Ian Anderson interview.

☆☆☆

However, let's say that you *do* happen to attend one of them and then somehow manage to buck the odds by graduating into a hack music reviewing job whose sole requirement is to faithfully spew out a publicist's promotional party line. If that happens, don't expect to receive any immediate remunerative under the table or below the belt gratuity for whatever pull-quote prowess you might happen to possess because that kind of payola-paying pocket-padding pandering doesn't come until later…*much* later. But spend a few years slavishly re-wording pedestrian press releases into comma-eschewing ungrammatical alliterative run-on sentences and you just might find yourself a few rungs up some flack's ladder and one step closer to life on Queasy Street.

☆☆☆

Or, you could follow Jeffrey Morgan's exemplary example and resolve instead that your career goal is to be a rock critic with integrity who always tells the facts and names the names, no matter what the personal or professional cost—and as this long-overdue authorized autobiography ably attests, that's not a bad legacy to leave behind. But it won't come easy because it never is easy walking down the road of rock 'n' roll righteousness. To get where you want to go you'll have to wade knee-deep through the dire depths of rock's sonic sewer, relying only on your own wits and—if you're lucky—a nocturnal retinue of bellhops; call girls; and tipsters who, hopefully, will help steer you in the right direction.

☆☆☆

You'll make a lot of enemies along the way. But look behind the shallow façade of every jealous hater who tries to tear you down with an unwarranted cheap smear or an illegally withheld paycheck and you'll find nothing but a lonely frustrated failure who would secretly give everything he or she owns just to follow in your footsteps, however fleetingly. So when the day comes that you find yourself the target of one of these effete elitist's ignorantly vicious attacks—and you will—just remember that all such resentment is pathetically borne out of the tragic nadir of their own morally and ethically inadequate souls, which are woefully bereft of any artistic aptitude and aesthetic merit.

Because life is the way we audition for God.

Let us pray that we all get the job.

— Lyle Rogers and Chuck Clarke, "Dangerous Business"

Machine Rock

MACHINE ROCK *has been making good on veiled threats since 1975. His review of* 1970: The Complete Fun House Sessions *appears in* The Stooges: The Authorized And Illustrated Story, *which is published by Abrams.*

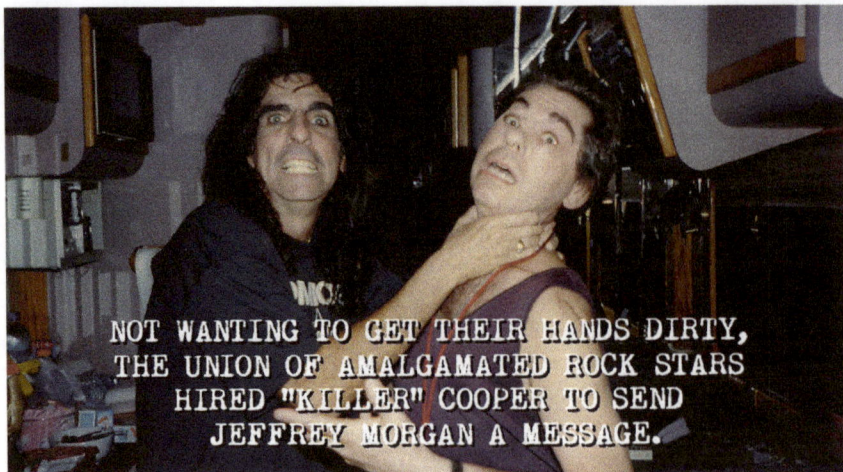

NOT WANTING TO GET THEIR HANDS DIRTY, THE UNION OF AMALGAMATED ROCK STARS HIRED "KILLER" COOPER TO SEND JEFFREY MORGAN A MESSAGE.

Oddly enough, although I did indeed end up interrogating Lou Reed and Ian Hunter and Patti Smith and Bob Dylan, amongst many others, not once did I ever ask them any of these questions. A classic case of life not imitating art.

A ROCK STAR'S GUIDE TO ROCK CRITICISM

While we're busy celebrating 25 years of rock 'n' roll, let us not forget that this year also commemorates the first quarter century of rock *criticism*. That's right: rock critics the world over have their *own* drum to bang this year—and, if we expect today's musicians to produce bigger and better music during the next 25 years, there's no reason why they can't also be expected to assist today's rock critics as they make an equal effort to upgrade the state of *their* art a couple of notches before 2004 rolls around.

And if you don't think they need to, think again.

Just a while back, Freddie Mercury accosted me during a New York City ballet performance, lividly demanding to know why he was always getting the short shrift in CREEM. "Surely it's not my attitude?" he preened. "I mean, we *rock 'n' roll*, don't we? What is it? My clothes? My teeth?"

In a somewhat similarly related incident, an equally distraught Keith Emerson was overheard asking why he always came off foul-smelling in interviews. "Why me?" he simpered.

Even Lou Reed (who's been into S&M relationships for years) broke down during a recent bull (and how) session,

confiding, "How come I look so bad in print every time I open my mouth?"

The answer to these questions is obvious. The fault, dear Brutus, lies not with the rock critics, but rather with the rock stars themselves. They may be whiz kids in the studio or on a well-lit stage, but get them in front of a microphone and they invariably end up being their own worst enemies.

No musician can afford to make easily avoidable—but potentially very costly—mistakes during rock interviews; interviews which, it should be remembered, are the staple of any self-respecting rock magazine.

Here then, for the Freddies, Keiths, and Lous of the profession, are the Seven Deadly Rock 'n' Roll Sins as committed by rock stars during rock interviews which cause such problems as well as how to avoid them:

☆☆☆

The rock star tries to avoid answering specific questions. Oh, he may *hear* the critic's question, but you can be sure that if he doesn't want to answer it, the rock start will act as if he *didn't*, choosing instead to change topics in mid-stream. They key is to answer all the rock critic's questions. Failure to do so will make the

rock star look evasive in print:

CREEM: What about all the oral sex references in your lyrics?

IAN HUNTER: Can I get you a cup of coffee?

CREEM: Do you realize you've used the word *suck* 83 times in your songs? What's with the obvious fixation?

IAN HUNTER: Nice weather we're having, isn't it?

☆☆☆

The rock star doesn't say anything quotable during the interview. He may even resort to platitudes, a direct result of his not having developed any carefully researched or fresh statements:

CREEM: You're just an old man. Why don't you pack it in and give up?

MICK JAGGER: No comment.

CREEM: Listen, did you and Keith *really* push Brian into that swimming pool?

MICK JAGGER: No comment.

☆☆☆

The rock star doesn't give the rock critic any news. Let's face it: rock critics are, essentially, reporters. And like all reporters they need information which hasn't been reported previously. A rock star can make a friend for life of the rock critic to whom he gives an exclusive story. To do otherwise is to waste the critic's valuable time:

PATTI SMITH: Y'know, I'm going to Paris next month with William Burroughs and Amanda Lear to raise the ghost of James Dean during an all-night séance.

CREEM: Didn't I read about that in several magazines a couple of months ago?

PATTI SMITH: Probably.

☆☆☆

The rock star tries to shade the truth. There's nothing a rock critic dislikes more than a rock star who tries to con his way through an interview. As always, direct honesty is always the best policy. Dishonesty (not to be confused with sensationalism), on the other hand, is

always a drag:

CREEM: What's this about Brian Eno producing your next album?

BOB DYLAN: Well, it's possible I can use any producer.

CREEM: Yes, but it's been pretty widely rumored that you're going to have Eno produce it, what with him staying at your house and all.

BOB DYLAN: There's always the possibility, but don't count on it. There have been rumors about me using Eno and I know I'm not going to do that.

CREEM: You really are a scam artist. You know that, don't you?

BOB DYLAN: No comment.

☆☆☆

The rock star tries to go off-the-record without the rock critic's permission to do so. Nothing is more damaging for a rock star than to be quoted in an interview as saying something which, at the time, he had assumed was going to be strictly off-the-record. Rock stars should *never* take anything for granted when being interviewed: if you want something to be off-the-record, get it in writing. Remember, there hasn't been a rock critic born (and make no mistake about it: they're born, not made) who's been afraid of the word sensationalism.

☆☆☆

The rock star insists on talking about subjects which are of absolutely no interest to anyone. This includes religion and politics (sexual or otherwise), both of which have nothing to do with rock 'n' roll.

☆☆☆

The rock star says things with a mistaken notion that he'll be able to see the story before it appears in print and get a second chance to edit his comments. (At least it won't happen in *this* magazine — Ed.) To the rock critic, there's no such thing as a second chance. If the rock star talks candidly about his affiliation with the American Nazi Party and hasn't stipulated beforehand that such comments be stricken from the record, then he might as well start packing. Rock critics are a stubborn breed and will fight to the death for their right not to be compromised.

Besides, a little sensationalism now and then never hurt anyone.

NEXT MONTH: All about lawsuits.

— CREEM, June 1979

DAVID BOWIE & THE LOWER THIRD
- "Can't Help Thinking About Me"
(Pye single deleted) ::

Q: What was Bowie singing while Lou was recording "Heroin" and "I'm Waiting For The Man" for the Velvets' first album? A: "Remember when we used to go to church on Sundays? I lay awake at night terrified of school on Mondaysmy girl calls my name, 'Hi Dave'" No wonder it's deleted. Next.

CREEM, August 1975

ENO - Another Green World
(Island) ::

If *Here Come The Warm Jets* was Eno's getting-up-in-the-morning-and-getting-raring-to-go album and *Taking Tiger Mountain* was Eno's wide-awake-and-working-in-the-afternoon album, then this must be Eno's coming-home-after-work-and-relaxing-in-the-evening album. Very few vocals as Old Uncle Eeno slips into his smoking jacket and slippers and retires for the rest of the night. The lull before the storm.

— CREEM, March 1976

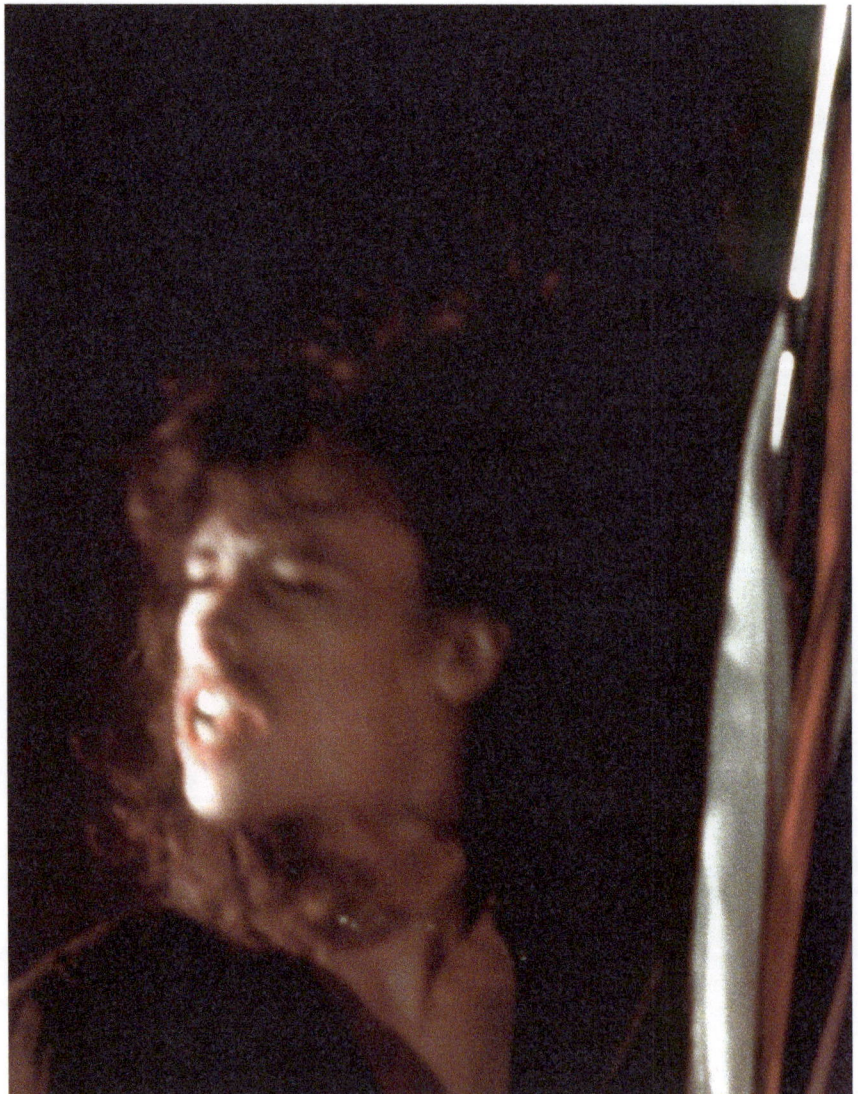

A ROCK STAR'S GUIDE TO ROCK PHOTOGRAPHY

LESSON 7: THE INSTRUMENT-ORIFICE INTERFACE

The rock star should always remember that his presence on stage means Open Season for the professional rock photographer, who will relentlessly stalk his prey hunting for that one unique visual moment which will forever live in infamy. Even the briefest of split-second transgressions will be caught on camera, so the rock star should always avoid penetrating his body by sticking a microphone into his mouth or by shoving a drumstick up his nose.

THE GOSPEL TRUTH
RICK WAKEMAN TESTIFIES

Best part of the job? Meeting your musical heroes and finding out they're even cooler in person than they are on record. And just like everyone else you'll encounter in Rock Critic Confidential, **Rick Wakeman** *is no exception.*

Anyone who thinks that Yes' current 35th Anniversary Tour is nothing but your predictable run of the mill cash grab reunion should read the group's entry in the 1981 edition of *The Harmony Illustrated Encyclopedia Of Rock.*

The first rude awakening is the list of then-current band members, which include Trevor Horn on vocals and Geoff Downes on keyboards. Next comes the group's history, which is littered with numerous tales of discontent and departure. Then, just in case you can't read between the lines, the entry concludes by spelling out the inevitable with a grim prediction: "1981 may well be recorded as the last year of Yes."

So don't go thinking that a 35th Anniversary Tour was by any means a sure thing because not only was Yes comatose and on life support for many years, even if it had survived, there was no guarantee of the following line-up surviving intact with it: Jon Anderson (vocals), Steve Howe (guitar), Chris Squire (bass), Alan White (drums), and Rick Wakeman (piano and synthesizers).

Now unless you're a die-hard Buggles fan, chances are you'll probably agree that the above-noted line-up is, indeed, the all-time classic configuration of Yes. But given their fragmented past, does the band think so as well? That's just one of the questions I put to Rick Wakeman backstage at the Air Canada Center when Yes recently came to Toronto.

Earlier that evening, I had arrived at the venue some 45 minutes prior to my scheduled interview time of 6:30. Nevertheless, I was promptly escorted to a dressing room where Rick Wakeman was already patiently waiting for me, even though the other band members had already gone back to their hotel an hour before.

During the course of the interview, Wakeman was as unstintingly gracious with his candid opinions as he was with his time—especially since he had less than an hour to get ready to go on stage by the time we were done. He's also extremely passionate when he talks about a subject that personally means a great deal to him. Which exactly is how our conversation began: spontaneously, before I even got a chance to ask the first question.

RICK WAKEMAN: I like Toronto a lot, it's a good city. The only thing that really annoys me about Toronto is that you're turning Maple Leaf Gardens into a grocery store, which is absolutely nothing short of disgusting. I mean how…

The people who run Toronto somehow can't see that in the music business and the entertainment business, there are about no more than four, possibly five, venues in the entire world that are synonymous with rock 'n' roll, the birth of rock 'n' roll, and all the things that happened to it.

Madison Square Garden is one. The Hollywood Bowl probably another. The Glasgow Apollo is another. And Maple Leaf Gardens is the other. It's absolutely synonymous with rock 'n' roll events.

Plus, if you take all the classic hockey games that have gone on there… I think you were one of the founding five or six—

JEFFREY MORGAN: "The Original Six."

WAKEMAN: I knew it was something like that. When you look at that building and think of all the classic things that have gone on there, you think: If ever there was a place where the politicians should have *one iota* of common sense… *That's* the place you should have your Canadian Hockey Hall Of Fame and your Canadian Rock Music Hall Of Fame.

Have some theatres in there that can show films all the time. Do things properly that the Americans *never* got right with Cleveland. Where you have cinemas, IMAX, the whole thing. People would come from all over the world to see that. It would be a huge, *huge* attraction if you put everything into it. It's perfect for that, you'd make it totally legitimate.

You could have theaters for concerts, you could have restaurants, you could have libraries; it would be absolutely unbelievable. And then do the same thing for the hockey team. Because you've *got* the place. I'll tell you what: in 25 years' time, people will be going: "Where's Maple Leaf Gardens?" "Oh, it's that grocery store around the corner."

It's unbelievably tragic. I get on my high horse about it because it's one of the few places… They knocked the place down in Glasgow, the Glasgow Apollo, which was synonymous with UK rock music probably more so than any other venue in Great Britain. Now there's a whole group of people who make pilgrimages to the site. And they're up in arms that it was knocked down: How could people knock part of the history of rock 'n' roll down?

MORGAN: That's why people go and stand on the parking lot where the Cavern Club used to be.

WAKEMAN: Exactly right! Now you look at the history of what's gone on in Maple Leaf Gardens; if anyone could make a list…

MORGAN: Sinatra, Elvis, Beatles, Stones, Dylan, Who…

WAKEMAN: Somebody one day has to point a finger at the town politicians, whoever they are, and say: "You should be *shot.*" Because if ever you had something that was gonna attract people from all over the world, that's it, sitting there. And you're gonna turn it into a grocery store. It stuns me.

I think there should be a plaque put up that says: "This famous building full of heritage and history was turned into a grocery store by the wankers who call themselves politicians for Toronto." Because one day—probably long after I'm dead and buried—the city will come to regret it.

But there you go, I've had my little bit. Fire away. Anything you like.

MORGAN: You played on David Bowie's first album and you played on Lou Reed's first album. You were a member of Strawbs and for the past 32 years you've been a member of Yes, on and off. So what I want to know is this: in the anthropology of rock 'n' roll—

WAKEMAN: *[laughs]*

MORGAN: —is Rick Wakeman the missing link between the glam rock era and the progressive rock era?

WAKEMAN: Well, I did all Marc Bolan's stuff as well. A lovely man. I did all T. Rex.

MORGAN: I was looking for a credit on his albums and couldn't find one.

WAKEMAN: I did a lot of—

MORGAN: The singles?

WAKEMAN: Yeah, I did "Ride A White Swan"… "Get It On"… In fact, at the time when Marc was really at his height, when T. Rex were just selling shed loads of stuff, I was sitting up at Regal Zonophone with him and Tony Visconti and Marc was having a huge argument with the record company. He was so fed up with them. And he had this song he wanted to record and, for whatever reason, the record company didn't want him to record it. And he said: "Sod it. I'm going into the studio, let's record it." And Tony Visconti, who was the producer, said: "Okay, but the record company won't release it."

So we went in and recorded this track. He only pressed up, I think it was 5000, and it came out under the band name 'Dib Cochran & The Earwigs.' And it was only way after his death that it came out that it was Marc. I wish I had one. I mean, they've been going for five thousand dollars on eBay if you can find one, they're so collectible.

But I'd play on everything from pop records to a lot of the glam stuff to rock stuff to classical stuff. I used to get called to do all those things, it was great. I really enjoyed it because I like people who are adventurous. When you sort of take away—and there's no pun intended—all the glam and glitter, you have to see what's left. And there's a lot of music left. And there were a lot of people like Lou Reed, people like Marc, who had a lot to offer, they were really very clever.

David Bowie is far and away the cleverest man I've ever worked with. Far and away. Absolute walking genius, David Bowie was, to work with. I did about two thousand sessions in four years, and of all those sessions the person I learned more from, was David.

MORGAN: In terms of music or attitude?

WAKEMAN: Both. Absolutely both.

MORGAN: Because he would've been around twenty at that time.

WAKEMAN: Yeah, he was in his early twenties. And he was just… Gosh, he was so far ahead of the game. He absolutely listened to nobody who he felt didn't have anything worth listening to. He wasn't into listening to

managers and record company executives. 'Cause his argument was: "If they want to be musicians, let them go and make a record, don't tell me what to do." And it was a wonderful attitude.

I can remember, in Trident Studios in London...how old was I... Crikey, it was 1969, I was twenty years old. In fact, when we recorded it, I was nineteen years old when we did "Space Oddity" originally because it was March 1969. I remember going into the studio, and we recorded it, did my mellotron bits, and walked up the stairs to go into the control room. And he was in there having a *blazing* row with the guy from Phillips, the record company guy. Because he wanted the single to be in stereo. And there weren't stereo singles then.

And he said: "This is stereo."

And the guy said: "No, we don't do stereo singles. Jukeboxes are in mono, everything's mono."

And David said: "I don't give a damn, this is stereo. In a little while, everything's going to be in stereo. There's going to be stereo jukeboxes. Everybody's going to have stereo at home, this has to be in stereo."

"Well, we're not geared up to press singles in stereo."

"You'd better *start* getting ready."

"Well, we're not going to do it!"

"Well, you don't have the single then!"

He fought and he was right. He was dead right and it was the first stereo single in the UK. And a massive monster. He was always one step ahead of the game.

He was always incredibly prepared in the studio. He said to me: "Never waste time in the studio. Studio time's really precious. Whilst you might have the money to waste in the studio now, there might be in years to come a time when you might wish you had that money. You'll look back at the time you wasted."

He never wrote in the studio, everything was already done. He was always what he called "75 percent prepared." You go in and he'd get the piece that far, and then the studio would take it that extra 25 percent. He respected the studio, and I think that's the one thing he taught me more than anything else: respect the studio. It's not a plaything.

He was light years ahead of his time, and it was an absolute pleasure to work with him. He respects what he can do more than anyone else I've ever met. Amazing character. Amazing man.

MORGAN: Speaking of memories and Maple Leaf Gardens, I saw you playing with Yes on the *Tales From Topographic Oceans* tour in 1973, and then I saw you a year later in 1974 during your own *Journey To The Center Of The Earth* solo tour. And I have to say, you seemed a lot happier playing your own music.

WAKEMAN: I love Yes dearly, but I didn't enjoy *Topographic Oceans*. At the time I actually said it was an over padded pile of shit. Those were the days when things were very black and white; we weren't mature enough to sit down and discuss things.

The truth of the matter is, I still don't like the album. There's a lot of very good things on it; there's some very good moments on it. But there's tons of padding. When we went in to do it, we had too much material for a single album. So you either made it into a double album—which means write a lot more stuff—or you just reduce the size and make it into a single album. The fact of life is, we went the wrong route and we didn't *have* any other material. So there was padding for *days* on it. And Yes had never done that and I *really* objected to it. *Vehemently* objected to it.

MORGAN: And that's why you ended up taking a walk for the first time.

WAKEMAN: Absolutely. We've all discussed it for a long time since then, and everybody actually agrees now that if the world of CD had been with us then, that problem would never have arisen. One track might've been eleven minutes, one might've been nine, one might've been twenty-six, one might've been fourteen. They would've had their natural length. It was an album that was eventually tailored and padded out to fit four sides of an album.

And I didn't like it. So I left.

MORGAN: Well, because you've left the band several times—

WAKEMAN: Actually, I only left twice. I left then, and then rejoined literally two years later for *Going For The One*.

And then I left with Jon in January 1980. Jon and I left at the same time.

We'd been in Paris and it was a shambles. It was just an absolute shambles. I mean, nobody was talking to anybody and everyone was fighting. The whole thing was just farcical. Then Alan went ice skating and broke his leg and we all pissed off. *[laughing]* It was really funny. It was very rock 'n' roll.

Nobody knew what to do with Yes! You've got a prog rock band that's coming into the big punk era. What the hell do you do with this band? Ahmet Ertegun had flown in and had wanted us to do a punk record and we told him to eff off.

So Jon and I'd had enough. We said, "That's it. This isn't what Yes is all about." And we both left. And they carried on. The Buggles came in and they did *Drama*. And then what happened was, at the end of the Eighties, the ABWH—Anderson Bruford Wakeman Howe—was formed.

It was *such* a mess because there was ABWH playing all the Yes stuff that we'd written. And there was what was lovingly known as "Yes West" on the west coast, which was basically Chris and Allan and Trevor and Tony. And the managements between them came up with this idea: Why don't we all join forces? Which, I have to say, for the stage show, was just fantastic.

But the album was just awful. I don't even classify it as a Yes album, the *Union* album. I always call it *Onion* because every time I hear it, it makes me cry. It was an absolute pile of junk because, basically, they wanted to get us out on the road really quick so they left this complete moronic *twat* to mix it. And, of course, it was the early days of computers, so he just basically wiped off things that Steve did, that I did, got his mates on, and it was a joke. It was an absolute *farce* of an album.

The tour was fantastic. But Steve, Bill and myself were told right at the beginning that the "Yes" name, which was owned by the Yes management people in California—and also Jon because, even though Jon was doing the ABWH, he still had an ownership in it—they said: "When the *Union* tour finishes, there's no way we want to keep an eight piece band going. So you, Bill and Steve will be surplus to requirements, so you can all go bugger off."

But what happened was, management

had gotten the mood of the Yes fans completely wrong, because the five that were left weren't the five that the fans wanted.

So as I say, I didn't leave.

MORGAN: Then let me put it this way: given the fact that you left twice over your principled beliefs, and that you're level headed about what's good and what's bad, would it be safe to say that you're the conscience of Yes?

WAKEMAN: *[smiling]* Um, to some extent. To some extent.

MORGAN: One of the big reasons why everyone could relate to you back then was because you were the only beer drinker in a band full of vegetarians.

WAKEMAN: Yeah, the meat eater.

MORGAN: And then you stopped drinking.

WAKEMAN: I stopped in '85. Oh yeah, I was a good drinker. Y'see, I was always a mug full of beer and skittles man, down at the pub playin' darts. The only reason I stopped drinking was because they told me… I mean, I had cirrhosis of the liver and alcoholic

hepatitis. And they said: You'll die. And I didn't really fancy the dying bit, so I stopped. I've got no objections to people who drink, and I still go down to the pub with my mates. Except I don't drink anymore.

MORGAN: Well, Alice Cooper's battles with the bottle are legendary—

WAKEMAN: Good man, Alice. He's a great guy.

MORGAN: —but ever since he stopped drinking, his albums and stage shows have been nothing short of phenomenal. So I was wondering if you can see any difference in your playing before and after—

WAKEMAN: I'm not saying I played badly, I never played badly. I'm not saying I went on stage drunk, but once you've gone completely clear headed, basically the music is your stimulant rather than anything else. But I listen to live recordings of things that I did back in the '70s and then how I've done things since. And there's no doubt about it: if I compare the two, it's like chalk and cheese.

Alice, in fact, is a real good mate of mine. Apart from the non-drinking thing, or the straightening out, the

other thing we have in common is that we're both huge fanatical golfers. In fact, we stood on the street last November in London—we were both staying at the same hotel, the Leonard, in London—and we were both leaving at the same time and it was really weird that we stood on the pavement discussing golf for about 45 minutes. Now, if anybody would have said to me years ago that Alice and me would be standing on the street in London discussing the merits of the PGA tour and how our golf game was… I mean, it was incredibly surreal. But that's what happens. *[laughs]* What happens to old rock 'n' rollers? They stop drinking and they start playing golf!

MORGAN: Recently Alice has been tackling some of the more serious issues going on in the world today, *vis-à-vis* good versus evil.

WAKEMAN: I'm biased, I'm a big Alice Cooper fan. I have been all the time. I think one of the good things that Alice is doing… It's great when you can think clearly enough to express yourself musically on how your thought patterns change and how you think. And if you can do that in a way that's still entertaining, then you've succeeded. And Alice succeeds in doing that. There's a lot of artists who try to put over their thoughts and words in music and it's thunderingly boring. But Alice is one of those who can do it in a very entertaining way.

MORGAN: You've always struck me as a spiritual person, yourself.

WAKEMAN: I am, yeah. I've got strong Christian views. I've had a huge faith all my life and I've not always been a good boy, I own up. And I know that if I ever manage eventually to get to the gates for God to tell me that He's not letting me in because I've been such a naughty boy, at least I can thank Him very much. I've got a strong faith, always have done, and that means a lot to me. It comes out in the music every now and then. It actually comes out by accident, sometimes.

It's really funny, I did an album called *Return To The Center Of The Earth*, which Ozzy sang on. I had Ozzy singing with the London Symphony Orchestra and the English Chamber Choir. It's a prog metal track played by a symphony orchestra. And there was a line in there that I never realized was in there until Ozzy pointed it out, which was: "The devil no longer has all the best tunes."

And Ozzy said: "Is that aimed at me then?"

And I said: "Absolutely not!"

It was just a coincidence, but so many people picked up on that and said: "You did that deliberately." I *didn't* do it but, yeah, spiritual lines come out every now and then. But I don't overtly do it deliberately.

"Rock 'n' roll is the devil's music!" Everyone knows that's not true. *Country and western* is the music of the devil. That's the *real* truth of the matter. My late Mother, bless her, loved country and western. God, I couldn't handle it.

MORGAN: Are you talking about the new pop country music or—

WAKEMAN: No, I'm talking about the old traditional thing where the only way you could walk out a room happy was if you played the record backwards so the dog came back to life and she moved back in the house. *[laughter]*

MORGAN: Dumb question time.

WAKEMAN: I like dumb questions. I've been married three times *and* divorced three times.

MORGAN: Are you aware of the fact that, in concert, Yes is the heaviest rock band of all time? Your live sound is just *massive*.

WAKEMAN: I'll tell you what's interesting… You know, this is really weird 'cause Jon and I were talking about it this morning. I would say twenty-five percent of all Yes fans were converted at gigs and not by record. It's a huge difference.

MORGAN: You guys are *monsterously* powerful live. "Heart Of The Sunrise"… "Yours Is No Disgrace"… "Perpetual Motion"… There are parts of those songs where you're just *brutal*.

WAKEMAN: That's what I mean. We do "And You And I" on this tour and it is a *hundred* times more powerful than the record version. The record version is very nice, it's almost twee. On stage it's *monster*.

MORGAN: In a battle of the bands, you'd beat Led Zeppelin, you'd beat Cream, you'd beat everyone.

WAKEMAN: Well, it is interesting, this band. It's a very strange… There's a few bands over the years who, for whatever reason, have had a certain line-up, however many there were in the band, that's added up to more than the total.

For example, if you take The Who when John Entwistle and Moonie were alive, those four together equaled *eight* when they were on stage. They were astonishing, those four. Zeppelin when Bonham was alive. Those four became seven or eight. The Beatles are a classic example. Those four became *fifty-eight*. And this particular line-up of Yes I classify as that. For whatever reason, it's not five ones is five, it's five ones is seven, eight, nine, ten.

MORGAN: It's the *only* line-up.

WAKEMAN: Yeah. It's the only one that works. It's weird, this particular

line-up. We are *aware* of it now. We realize there's just something…it's sort of strange to come to terms with it. When we got back together two and a half years ago, some of the stuff I hadn't played for twenty-five years. And we just sorta met and said, "What should we play?" And I said, well, let's do… I can't remember what piece it was, but we hadn't played it since 1979—and we just played it all the way through. It was just *really bizarre*. And it was like we'd never not ever played it before. And we all said afterwards: "Oh boy, *that's* a bit freaky."

It's like, Steve's on the other side of the stage and I'm on this side of the stage. Steve and I are really good friends, but we have completely different lifestyles so we don't socialize that much. But there's this really weird thing that happens when I know *exactly* what he's going to do at any given time and he knows exactly what *I'm* going to do at any given time. There's a weird sort of telepathy there that goes on that's really strange.

I've got it with Jon as well. We'll often look over and like sort of grin at each other. It's an X factor. There's an X factor that slips in and you can't define the X factor. And if you try and look at it or analyze what it is, then it'll all collapse. You just be very thankful that it's there.

I'm just grateful that we've all got our own hips. I mean, I look across the stage and it cracks me up that there we all are, five people that now weigh individually what we all used to weight in total back in 1971—with the exception of Steve, who's vegetarian, so he's like a brilliantine stick insect. There's nothing of him, but the rest of us is really funny.

MORGAN: All things considered, given the group's positive name and uplifting musical content, isn't Yes the perfect band for you to be in?

WAKEMAN: Oh it is, absolutely. You're absolutely right. The interesting thing is, during the periods of time that I wasn't in this band, I always felt that I was in it anyway. This wasn't a band

you could leave. Even the two times that I left, I never really felt like I left the band. It's very bizarre. It's like there's sort of an umbilical cord that stretches between us spiritually.

The lyrical content has been an interesting one because so many people have said: "Oh, a lot of Jon's lyrics are very New Age" or: "They're from another religion."

MORGAN: That reminds me, I was wondering if you can tell me what this means: "Yesterday a morning came, a smile upon your face. Caesar's Palace, morning glory, silly human race."

WAKEMAN: "Even *Siberia* goes through the motions." I have visions of thousands of Siberian men, all sittin' on the toilet in the morning. *[laughter]*

MORGAN: I'd like to thank you for ruining that song for me forever.

WAKEMAN: Cheers!

— **CREEM, June 2004**

LOU CAUSES RAT MELT-DOWN

Can guitar solos cause permanent neural damage? According to a recent government survey in which laboratory rats were subjected to over 2,000 different guitar solos through miniature headphones, the answer is yes.

Dr. David Ludden of the National Health Institute says in his report that the rats' test results were "almost identical" to those he received from various North American teenagers earlier in the month.

Of the 340 rats and 235 teenagers tested, only one guitar solo caused instantaneous fusion of the spinal cord in all 575 cases: Lou Reed's 1967 extended break on "I Heard Her Call My Name," which Dr. Ludden calls "a killer."

The four runners-up for the most damaging psychotic guitar solos ever recorded were Keith Richards ("Sympathy For The Devil," 1968), James Williamson ("Shake Appeal," 1973), Robert Fripp ("Baby's On Fire," 1973) and Phil Manzanera ("Third Uncle," 1974).

A rumor that Roger Corman has hired the rats and teenagers as extras to be featured in a low-budget remake of *Gimme Shelter* starring The Godz has yet to be confirmed.

— **CREEM, August 1979**

ALICE COOPER

DEBBIE HARRY

THE LOW SPARK OF THE RACCOON LODGE

STEVE WINWOOD
Roll With It
(Virgin)

FADE IN.

[Scene: The Kramden kitchen. Ralph sits at the center table reading a newspaper. The door opens and Norton enters, carrying a Sony Walkman.]

NORTON: Hey Ralphie-boy, what's doin'?

RALPH: Don't interrupt me, I'm checking my lottery numbers.

[Norton sits next to Ralph, puts on his headphones and turns on the Walkman. Loud music leaks from the headphones and Norton starts humming even louder. Ralph tries to ignore Norton at first and then looks at him, steamed. Finally he gives him a shot in the arm.]

RALPH: *Will* you cut it out? Didn't I say I was trying to concentrate? What *is* that anyway?

NORTON: It's my new Walkman. I gave my old one to Trixie. All the guys in the sewer use 'em.

RALPH: Walkman, huh? Well, what are you listening to?

NORTON: *A Date With Elvis.*

RALPH: Mind if I listen?

NORTON: Be my guest.

[Norton puts the headphones on Ralph and turns on the Walkman. Immediately loud music leaks from the headphones. Ralph jumps up, tears the headphones off his head and hops around the table, holding his ears.]

RALPH: GAAAAAAAAAA! YEAAAAAAGH! EAUGHHHHHH! *[slugging Norton]* What are you, crazy? Do you want to *deafen* me? Why is that so loud?

NORTON: You think *that's* loud, you oughtta try working in a *sewer* sometime!

RALPH: That is the *worst* Elvis Presley album I've ever heard.

NORTON: Elvis Presley? *[laughs]*

That's not Elvis Presley! That's *The Cramps!*

RALPH: *[looks at cassette tape, then points to Norton]* You are a mental case. Haven't you got anything *else* I can listen to?

NORTON: Just the new Steve Winwood tape, but Trixie's upstairs wrapping it up to give to Haggerty's wife for a wedding present.

RALPH: *[eyes bulging, banging table]* Wedding present! Wedding present! Norton! I'm in big trouble! Big trouble! *[runs hand through hair]* Tomorrow is me 'n' Alice's wedding anniversary and I didn't get her anything! She'll *kill* me if I don't get her something! What am I gonna do?

NORTON: Why don'tcha get her a Walkman?

RALPH: *[brightening]* Norton! That's a *great* idea! Alice is *always* complaining about being lonely during the day! A Walkman'd be *perfect!*

NORTON: *[chuckling]* Yeah, now she can make pot roast listening to The Cramps!

RALPH: What are you, *nuts?* What about the Steve Winwood tape? What's wrong with *that?*

NORTON: Absolutely nothing, Ralph. Of course, *Roll With It* is no *Date With Elvis*, but Winwood is big and gonna be bigger than ever once this one hits the airwaves. Just like Sting and Robbie Robertson, not to mention George Harrison, this latest by Winwood is strictly designer music all the way…which isn't to say that he doesn't get it up once or twice: the title track is a funky example of Steve thinking with his hips, while "Holding On" is another example of Winwood's Pete Townshend *Miami Vice* style.

Radio loves this guy and the girls think he's strictly va-va-va-voom all the way, but if the guys listened to this in the sewer, they'd be nodding off and drowning in droves.

Don't worry, Alice'll love it—and Cassidy can get a deal on both the Walkman and the tape. I'll have them for you tomorrow, Ralph, gift wrapped and ready to go.

RALPH: Norton, you're a real pal.

[Scene: The Kramden kitchen the next night. Alice is at the stove when Ralph enters, carrying his lunch box and a paper bag.]

RALPH: Hi'ya, Alice.

ALICE: Oh, hi Ralph. Dinner'll be in a few minutes. *[turning around]* What's in the bag, Ralph?

RALPH: *[sheepishly]* Well, I—uh… *[hands bag to Alice]* Happy anniversary, Alice.

ALICE: *[taking bag]* Ralph, you remembered! *[pulls out box and removes wrapping]* Oh, Ralph! A Walkperson!

RALPH: *[proudly]* Now you won't have to be lonely while I'm at work, Alice. *[absently nodding his head]* There's a tape in there too, Alice.

ALICE: [opening the *Walkman*] A *Date With Elvis!* Oh, Ralph!

RALPH: *[does double take]* What? Gimme that! *[grabs tape and stares at it, eyes bulging and very steamed]* Wait'll I get my hands on that Norton. *[sweating bullets and wiping his mouth with his hand]* Look Alice, I—uh…

ALICE: Ralph, how did you know I love The Cramps?

RALPH: I'm awfully sorry about the— *[does take]* —you do? Oh, yeah, *yeah* . . . *[swaggers and nods head]*

ALICE: Now I don't have to borrow Ed's copy anymore. Aren't you wondering what I got *you*, Ralph?

RALPH: Yeah, Alice, I'm wondering.

ALICE: First, I made your favorite dinner, pot roast. Second, I got us two tickets to see Steve Winwood at the Bensonhurst Hall. And third… *[she whispers in his ear]*

RALPH: *[beaming, snaps fingers]* Baby, you're the greatest!

EMBRACE AND KISSVILLE.

FADE OUT.

— CREEM, July 1988

JUDGEMENT AT OSTERBERG
THE STOOGE SELLS OUT

IGGY POP
Iggy's Greatest Commercials
($immons Records)

Ever since he signed with Gene $immons, Iggy's career has been one long concrete kissing belly flop into the shallow end of the consumerism pool. So it comes as no surprise that this craven cash grab opens up with "Lust For Life Insurance!" and then spews out every other crass commercial from Iggy's sixty second song book, including ads for:

Raw Power Energy Drinks! Shake Appeal Body Spray! Penetration Condoms! Death Trip Funeral Parlors! My Idea Of Fun Amusement Parks! Dynamite Boogie Booze! I Wanna Eat Your Dog Food! Cock In My Pocket Vibrators! Skull Ring Tones! Mexican Guy Immigration Lawyers! I Need More Credit Loans! Cold Metal Coffins! Blah Blah Blah Phone Cards! ATM Bank Machines! Eggs On Plate Frozen Dinners! Sell Your Love Escorts! I Got A Right Legal Services! Tight Pants Jeans! Trollin' GPS Units! Lucky Monkeys Lotteries! Heavy Liquid Plumber! Gimme Some Skin Moisturizer! Head On Auto Repair! I Need Somebody Matchmakers! Born In A Trailer Parks! Wet My Bed Diapers! She Took My Money Divorce Attorneys! I'm Fried Chicken Wings! TV Eyeliner! Your Pretty Face Is Going To Hell Beauty Salons!

Has the man *no* shame?

— CREEM, May 2007

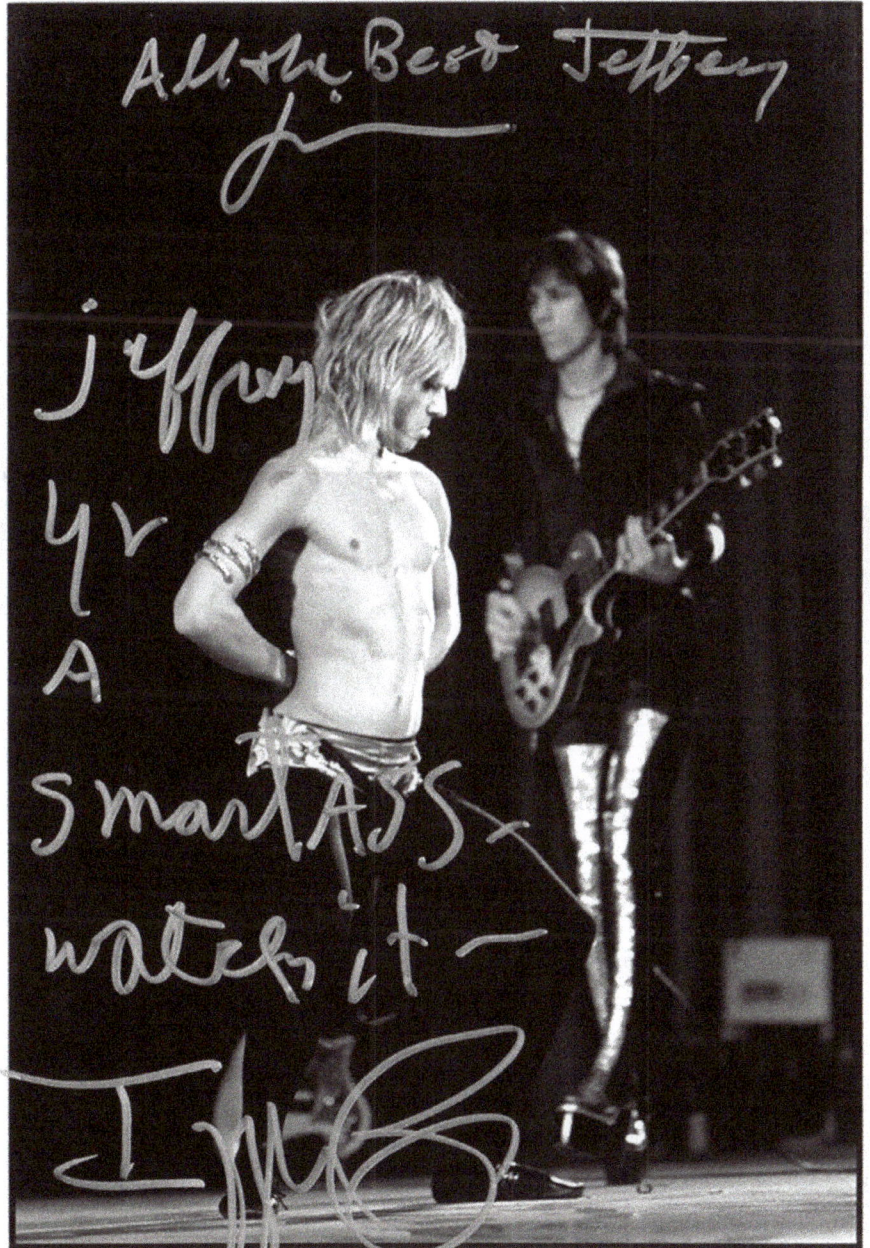

Photo: © Robert Matheau

VICTORY THEATRE
287 SPADINA AVENUE   TORONTO, ONT.
FRIDAY EVENING AT 8:00
S. R. O. PROMOTIONS PRESENT
"IGGY"
PRICE $4.00 + .40 — $4
JAN. 25 — E.
$4.40
JAN. 25

Once upon a midnight dreary in the bleak December, not a creature was stirring until there came a tapping at my chamber door. Quoth the Raven: "It's for you."

THE NIGHT BEFORE CHRISTMAS WITH JETHRO TULL

IAN ANDERSON TALKS TURKEY

JEFFREY MORGAN: Merry Christmas!

IAN ANDERSON: Merry Christmas to you!

MORGAN: And thanks for the enjoyment that I've had listening to your music over almost forty years of Jethro Tull.

ANDERSON: Wow. That makes you an old guy.

MORGAN: It makes me an old guy of about 52 and a half years old.

ANDERSON: Oh, *okay!* Well, that half gets even more important when you get older.

MORGAN: Y'know, if they can ever find a way for you to get royalties from people who hum music or sing it out loud at inopportune times—

ANDERSON: You'd owe me lunch!

MORGAN: And a couple of drinks. Now what's all this about you claiming not to be a good singer? Surely you must know that, whatever you may lack in technical proficiency, you more than make up for in personality and humor. I mean, you're one of the most distinctive and personable performers in the entire history of rock 'n' roll.

ANDERSON: Well, I think that what I was probably getting at is that, for some people, singing is very natural and—

MORGAN: You may have to *work* at it, but—

ANDERSON: Yeah, well, that's the problem, you see. Having become the singer in a band basically because no one else could sing at all, I had to make due with what I had. And it's always

been…it's never been *easy* for me to sing. I've never found it to be a particularly…*natural* thing to do, somehow. I mean, I *do* have a passion for performing the music and the songs that I write, but I think that if I could have been given one gift in life, it would've been to have had an *easy* vocal style. That's what I *do* detect in some people that I regard as good singers because for them singing is a very natural expression and natural extension of what they do. Whereas for me, it's a bit of a wrestling match, really, with some limited physical prowess that I have. I know what I *want* to sing, it's in my *head* and, for the most part, I kinda *get* there, but it's just not easy. It's always been something that I felt I had to kinda *work* at harder than most other people, whose singing voices I admire.

MORGAN: But there are *so* many people these days who have the technical proficiency but don't have a *fraction* of the vitality and personality that *you* have.

ANDERSON: And there are also some that are just atrociously awful singers, y'know. I mean, one thing that I find extremely off-putting is when there are accolades heaped upon certain people who sing grotesquely out of tune a lot of the time. And that I find quite amazing that they've managed to continue being recognized. There are a couple of people, who I won't mention, who're… I suppose quite… I mean, that's what they do. That's *all* they do, is sing. It's not like they can fall back on strumming a guitar or playing some amazing piano or something.

But a couple of people that I regard as *really* poor singers have made *very* substantial pots of millions out of doing what they do, in *my* view, really badly. On *top* of which, what *really* grates on my ears, is when singers from *my* side of the world feel *compelled* to sing in fake American accents as soon as they open their mouths to sing, whilst the rest of the time they speak in their native voice; their regional British accents. I've always found it *really* quite puzzling why the *American* accent, as the sum form of pop and rock music, has to extend everywhere—as it, unfortunately, pretty much always does. I mean, there *are* exceptions like, I suppose, David Bowie who, for the most part, has managed to sing in something resembling his own voice.

MORGAN: Except in the early days, when he was pretending to be Anthony Newley.

ANDERSON: Well, except, actually, that really was closer to David Bowie…that *is* closer to the way he *was*. Anthony Newley was, in fact, a very close…again, he was one of those guys who just…one of the few people who *did* sing in his natural voice. And I think I've always admired *those* people, who managed to do that. There've been some like that in the UK, not necessarily very well known elsewhere, who've been able to make a career out of just singing in their real voice.

But it's those that adopt the *ridiculous* American *twang* of Elton John or Mick Jagger that I find *absolutely puzzling*. It

really is *downright puzzling*. I mean, even *Sting* does this rather American drawly kind of singing that's…it's a little weird, really. I've never understood why they feel they have to *do* that. I mean, paying *homage* to the origins of rock music as being truly American is one thing, but to *ape* this kind of American drawl seems to me rather weird. Anyhow, I mean we've all, I suppose, slipped into that bad habit from time to time, and some have slipped into it as a permanent…*frock* of their vocal performance, and that *does* puzzle me.

However, anyway, singing is singing and I'm one of those folks who, you know, as they say: jack of all trades, master of none. I'm a bit of a strummer, a flute player, a mandolin player, a singer, a… whatever. If it's there and it makes a not too dreadful noise, then I'll have a *go* at it.

MORGAN: In other words, you're number one in a field of one.

ANDERSON: Well, *yeah*. And you know that's, I suppose, what always *gripped* me about music in the *first* place, is the people that I admired were people who were fairly unique in their style. I've never really liked the *mainstream* performers in rock music. There're some whose abilities I greatly *admire* but, nonetheless, I wouldn't want to be *like* them. I mean, I greatly admire, for example, what I think was probably rock's finest tenor vocalist, which was Lou Gramm in Foreigner. I mean, I thought he was, certainly on record, a really brilliant singer with a bell-like

clarity and an ability to sing all the way up there without the histrionics of Ian Gillan and the other sort of, you know, heavy metal kind of falsetto vocalists. I mean, he had a *real voice*, Lou Gramm. Sadly, he doesn't have it anymore. But it's a great tool to have put to work so well.

However, I wouldn't want to try and sing like him. I *couldn't* sing like him, my voice is not in the same range. But it's possible to admire and respect people without wanting to *be like* them. And so I guess the folks that I've held up as examples of what I would *like* to do are the individualists: the Americans Frank Zappa and Captain Beefheart. And amongst the British contingent, there's really… [*laughs*] …really rather a *lot* of them over the years who are made in a mold—and then someone quickly destroyed the mold after the creature came to life.

MORGAN: I don't suppose I could talk you into mounting a touring road show of

A Passion Play to show those ABBA and Queen musicals what *real* rock theater would be like.

ANDERSON: [*laughs*] Well…

MORGAN: I mean, this *is* the ideal time.

ANDERSON: I think you just hit on the problem with my objections to anything like that because of the words *rock theatre*. There *was* a time when the idea of a more theatrical form of rock music *did* seem as if it was quite fitting. And I suppose in 1972 and 1973 it seemed to me that it was possible to do. But the trouble was that, while we went down that route ourselves—in a humorous way, I mean, it was never meant to be sort of *serious*; it was always meant to be a bit tongue in cheek and a bit *fun*…

MORGAN: Well, *some* of us got that.

ANDERSON: *Yeah!* Well, this was the era of Monty Python and the Flying Circus and it was all that surrealistic

British humor sort of finding an outlet. But the *theatricality* of it, after a couple of years, made me feel uncomfortable. Especially because…in the wake of that…I suppose…probably Alice Cooper 'round the same time as Jethro Tull was doing that kind of slightly theatrical approach to rock music.

But it seemed that very quickly people were jumping on that bandwagon and the big production tours started happening and people were going bigger and louder and brighter and it seemed somehow to get away from the spirit of what the music was about. And I think somewhere around that time I think I persuaded myself that, really, it was better to be minimizing the theatre to just the occasional use of props or *personality* kind of moments, rather than it being theatrical in the sense that there were stage sets and carpenters and electricians and all kinds of people you had to have along in order to put something together that became very calculated and very choreographed and scripted which was something that I didn't feel very good about. Because the improvisation aspect of playing music is something I've always felt should extend to the performance as a whole.

So I kinda went 180 degrees away from the theatrical side of presentation. But what I do *today*, I'm well aware that there's a theatricality in the way I present it. But it's really a theatricality in personality terms rather than involving other people or involving other elements of presentation. I mean, big, glitzy productions are just something that make me feel uncomfortable.

MORGAN: Did you ever get to see Roland Kirk perform live?

ANDERSON: We actually *played* on the same bill with Roland Kirk, *right* at the very beginning of Jethro Tull's career in America. I think one of the very first concerts we played, probably the second or third show we ever played in the USA, was the Newport Jazz Festival and Roland Kirk was on the bill and briefly we were introduced. And I was quite nervous to meet him because, number one, he was black—and I wasn't. Number two, he was, even at that point, I think, seriously involved in Islam—and I wasn't. And he was blind—and I wasn't. He was also a proper jazz musician who understood the nuances of jazz and the constructions of jazz in a way that I didn't, don't, and never will.

So he was a really kind of different kettle of fish to *me* and I found him quite gracious and pleasant, and he was aware that I played and recorded a piece of his music. And I think he was mildly flattered by that, as most people are when they hear someone has done one of your songs. I'm not sure that we were actually able to hear him play live on that occasion because of just the scheduling of things and where we had to be or what time we were on or what have you. I'm pretty sure he didn't see *us* play live, either, but it was kind of interesting to have been around him.

The same thing happened with Captain Beefheart, actually. I saw him back in 1968 I guess—maybe late '67 or early '68—on a visit to London. And at that time I was mildly amused by him but thought he was a faker and a sham—as, indeed, to a large extent he *was*. But later on, I think at his most fruitful period of music around '72, '73, toward the end of his days with the best lineup of the Magic Band, he did produce some really, really sterling work. I think from *Trout Mask Replica* through to *The Spotlight Kid*, it was a great, great time. And I'm very pleased to have met and known him

in '72. He was a medicine man. He was the guy that sold snake oil from the back of a covered wagon. He was a charming rogue, but he was… He had been struck by the wand of genius and did have an amazing ability with words and emotions which I think was a strong but, ultimately, *indirect* influence on me. I mean, again, not someone I would ever want to try to imitate particularly, although I think, perhaps, one of my very early songs, "A Song For Jeffrey," was one slightly, *slightly* orientated towards a kind of Captain Beefheart feel—albeit at that time I hadn't met him.

MORGAN: Where do you keep your heavy metal Grammy?

ANDERSON: Well, funnily enough, *it just cropped up!* The day before yesterday *I discovered it!* I've said repeatedly for some years *I've no idea where it is.* I remember *having* it and sort of looking at it and thinking: umm, right, yes, not the sort of thing you would put on the mantelpiece for the neighbors to look at when they came 'round. I mean, it's an *accolade* to've won a Grammy, but as an object to sort of *display in your house*, it looks a bit tacky and a bit *whoops*. You wouldn't kinda wanna… *I* wouldn't wanna put it on display, but then you won't…you don't find gold albums and things hanging around my house, either. Or awards or whatever.

I was awarded a Doctorate in Literature, but it's still a piece of paper wrapped up in a tube somewhere in a pile of paperwork in my office here. It's not that I don't *value* it, but I just don't… I'm not

one of those people who feels it necessary to put it on the wall. [*laughs*] I don't need to be reminded of who I am or what I've done. Hopefully my memory's sufficient to keep me with a sense of what accomplishments I've managed without having to put them on the wall to remind me. I don't have to show them off in some kind of a way. I don't feel comfortable about that.

So, yes, I *did* discover the Grammy. It showed up because we had an insurance evaluation going on in the last week, and so we had some various experts in silver and jewelry and furniture and paintings, whatever, swarming over the house making notes and taking photographs of everything because it was time to renew our household insurance contents and we had to do a complete reevaluation of everything because we hadn't done one for a long time.

So in that search, one of the chaps said: "Oh, by the way, I saw your Grammy." I said: "*No!* Where did you see *that?*" He said: "It's in a case in one of the rooms upstairs. We saw it." I said: "Show me where it is." So he took me to it and, sure enough, the Grammy award was in some obscure part of the house that *I* never go in, in a bookcase somewhere. Not really obviously visible unless you opened it up and looked inside. *So now I know where it is.* But it's *still* not coming out on public display!

— **previously unpublished, 2005**

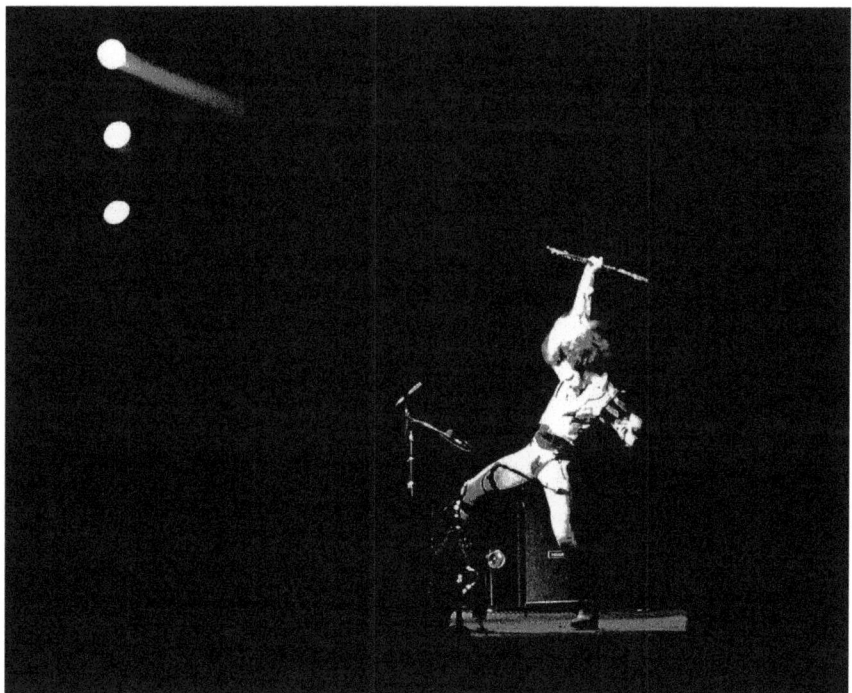

CAREER ADVICE FROM STAN LEE

Stan Lee & Jeffrey Morgan 1970 - Photo Credit - Joe Morgan.

The first time I met Stan Lee was in 1968 at "Captain" George Henderson's *Triple Fan Fair*, which was Toronto's first comic book convention. I was 14 at the time while Stan, at 45, was figuratively *and* literally "The Man" who was on top of the comic book world. But I knew my stuff and Stan *knew* that I knew, which is why we could stroll down Bloor Street talking shop while others trailed in our wake.

Two years later I was sitting on the couch in Stan's office at Marvel Comics in New York, showing him samples of my artwork. When he was finished, Stan looked up at me. "So you want to work in comic books," he said. "Well, I wouldn't if I were you. *It's not a very nice business.*"

Then he paused and leaned forward. "You know, my wife and I recently moved out to a new place in Long Island," he confided. "And every month the office sends out to the house a big box containing all of the comics that we put out that month. And they *keep* sending them out, month after month, and the boxes are piling up, unopened, and my wife is always after me to get *rid* of them. But I *can't* because *they've all got my name in them!*"

Two years after that, I met Stan for a third time. But it was during our fourth meeting in 1975 that I gave him copies of the photographs taken at our first two encounters, one of which bore an inscription stating that he was my greatest influence as a writer.

Which remains true to this day. I intuitively knew that Stan's informally ornate off-the cuff and over-the-top huckstering soapbox style, wherein ten words were always used where one would suffice, was perfectly suited for what I had to say as a rock critic—especially since I had already been using my own customized version of Stan's rapid-fire repartee for years while writing essays about music and movies all throughout high school and university.

Which explains why *Cahiers du Cinéma* critic and film studies professor Robin Wood felt compelled to accurately assess me as having "*a magazine style of writing, if that's what you aspire to.*" He may have meant it as a withering warning, but it was one of the best compliments I ever received.

As for Stan's sagacious advice, I decided instead to heed Fred

Flintstone's earlier assessment of my artwork and continued to pursue my artistic dream, even after getting comic strip rejection slips from both *Rolling Stone* and CREEM in the same year. Eventually a comic book series of mine called "The Studio" *did* get published monthly in *Vortex* magazine where, ironically, it caught the ever-discerning eye of Stan's legendary secretary at Marvel, "Fabulous Flo" Steinberg.

But it wasn't until Dark Horse Comics published my 320 page mystery graphic novel *The Brides Of Mister X And Other Stories* in a deluxe hardcover edition that I finally found my true comic book calling—not as an artist, but as a writer.

I'm sure Stan would've approved.

— previously unpublished, 2021

Stan Lee & Jeffrey Morgan 1968 - Photo Credit - Jeffrey Morgan archive.

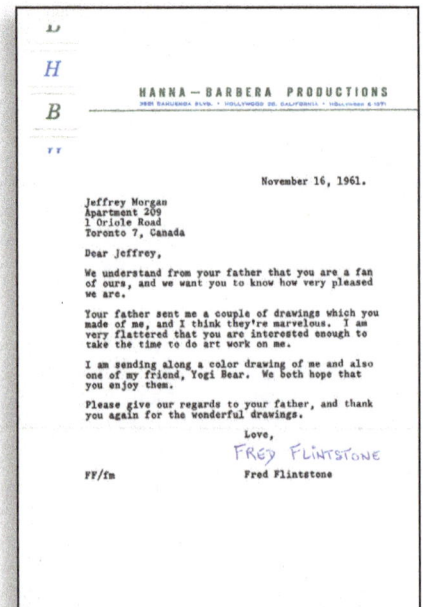

Fred Flintstone letter - Jeffrey Morgan archive.

IGGY POP

Greetings, my friend. You are interested in the unknown, the mysterious, the unexplainable. That is why you are here. And now, for the first time, we are bringing to you the full story because we cannot keep this a secret any longer. My friend, can you prove that it didn't happen?

THE SECRET LIFE OF AMANDA LEAR

She's been called everything from the Renée Richards Of Rock to Miss Before And After Science Of 1984. And although she's sold millions of albums in Europe and is that country's reigning white disco queen, North Americans probably know Amanda Lear best as the cover girl on Roxy Music's *For Your Pleasure* album or as the is-she-or-isn't-she host(ess) of David Bowie's 1973 *Nineteen-Eighty Floor Show* television special.

In the interim between then and now, she's recorded two albums (*I Am A Photograph* and *Sweet Revenge*), the second of which has recently been released domestically. A third, *Never Trust A Pretty Face*, can be expected shortly.

Still, it's always been Amanda's dubious sexual history which has captured the imagination of most people so, when the man herself came to town as part of a promotional tour, I decided to clear up the mystery once and for all.

The reader is invited to draw his or her own conclusions.

*** *** ***

AMANDA LEAR: What would you like to know about myself? Who I am, for a start, and how I came to this lousy profession? I was a late '60s child wearing mini skirts, smoking dope like everybody else.

JEFFREY MORGAN: How did you get involved with David Bowie?

LEAR: One day, I went on my own to see David Bowie and I offered him my lyrics, my songs. And I said: "Would you like to sing my songs?" and he said: "No, but I'm doing a show for NBC, would you like to be in it?" and I said, "But doing what?" And he said: "I like the stuff you write, you write funny things. Why don't you write my dialogue? Because I'm Ziggy Stardust, therefore I don't talk to the audience. So what you do is write my dialogue and we'll talk together."

But I wanted him to sing my songs and he said: "Why don't you sing them yourself?" and that's how it started. From then on he sent me to singing classes for about six months and by the end of 1974 I was signed up by his record company—MainMan—and I was ready to record, with him to produce my first record. And that's when I left.

MORGAN: Why?

LEAR: They said: "You're going to be our next big star if you'll just wait. We'll pay your rent, you just sit around while we train you. You'll go to dance class and everything. This year we're going to concentrate on Mick Ronson and then we're going to concentrate on Dana

Gillespie." Where are they now? Whatever happened to Mick Ronson and Dana Gillespie? Nothing. In the meantime, I've sold three million records. So, in fact, the best move I ever made was to leave his bloody company.

MORGAN: Speaking of good moves, Lou Reed once described you as: "A fabulous sex change…a real piece."

LEAR: All this publicity is my own doing, as you know very well. I'm the first one to publicize myself and those things.

MORGAN: Are they true?

LEAR: I'm the one who *started* the rumor, darling. Not them. I mean, I'm the one who *made* Lou Reed—

MORGAN: But when people read what Lou Reed says, or what some hack in *Swank*—

LEAR: *I'm* the one who tells *Swank*. *I'm* the one who tells those people. I'm the one who knows Amanda Lear better than anyone else in the world.

MORGAN: But Amanda Lear is never quoted in those magazines. It's always second-hand writers who end up giving their own opinions…

LEAR: That's because Amanda Lear has got a good P.R. You see, when Amanda Lear became a product we decided we had to sell Amanda Lear, right? Now, how are we going to sell her? This is Amanda Lear. It is not a terribly attractive product. So we've got to make it attractive, we've got to make it so people will *die* to buy it.

She's a blond model who sings? Nobody's interested.

She's a new disco singer? Who cares?

Now, if you're going to say about Amanda Lear that she is a *transsexual*… *That* might get some response, you see.

And if we're going to say that Amanda Lear was a girl friend of David Bowie, Lou Reed, Tom Jones—I don't know, whatever—all made up stories 'cause the only things that sell are made up stories, as you know since you're a writer.

MORGAN: So they're *all* made up stores?

LEAR: Absolutely. But they sold. We got an instant response. As Amanda Lear, a singer, nobody was interested. Now, as Amanda Lear, a *personality… Strange woman…* It created an image. It created an impact. People *love* the story. It got me onto TV talk shows and everything, I did a nude centerfold for *Playboy*; everybody saw the whole thing was not true. I mean, *Playboy* doesn't usually have naked gentlemen in their pages. I've been in thousands and thousands of magazines in the nude or clothed. The whole of Europe and the world knows all those stores were gimmicks.

So what happens to me, as a disco singer especially, is that I have to make Amanda Lear really interesting so that when Amanda Lear will not be a disco singer anymore but will sing *Godspell*, or whatever, then the people will still buy her records. So what happens is that all those kids in Germany, or wherever, are in love with Amanda Lear. *Not* with "Follow Me," "The Queen Of Chinatown," all my hits—they're in love with *Amanda*. It's *Amanda's* poster that's on the wall.

Even now that all those kids are masturbating, saying: "Yeah, she's a woman, there is a picture, naked," it doesn't matter. Still you have to maintain some kind of arrogance because it's part of my image.

MORGAN: What *about* all those nude photos?

LEAR: I must never, ever again—it was a big mistake, in fact. Take all my clothes off in magazines—that's *wrong*. Because, in fact, people don't *want* that from me. They do not want to be confronted with a close-up of my pussy. They want to *dream*. Amanda Lear is a *fantasy* for those people. On this record sleeve, why am I dressed like that? It's not that in real life I walk around in black leather and whips—*thank God*, for my neighbors…

*** *** ***

NEXT MONTH: The truth about Jerry Hall.

— **CREEM, February 1979**

DAVID BOWIE

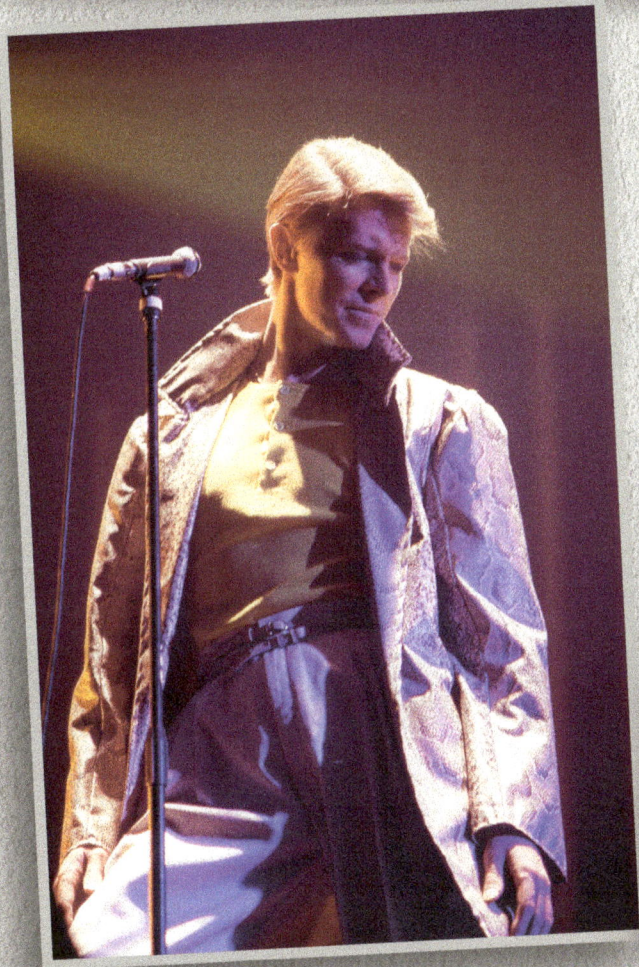

Mortified that I'd momentarily been duped by a phony CREEM record review of Lou Reed Sings Gilbert And Sullivan, *I promptly wrote my own fake review and mailed it to Lester Bangs purely as a joke. The joke was on me, however, when Lester actually published my privately submitted goof as a feature record review under my own byline. Then the joke was on the ever-insecure Pete Townshend, who couldn't allow himself the luxury of belief when I told him that the review was my good-natured way of thanking him for* Quadrophenia.

Thirty-one years later, when his record company asked me if there was anything that I'd like to ask Pete while he was promoting The Who's new album, I couldn't resist giving that big schnozz one more friendly tweak...

YOU CAN'T KEEP A GOOD BOOK DOWN
CHAPTER ONE, VERSE 1975
PETE FILLS A SCRIPTURE

THE WHO
Bible One
(MCA)

Just when you think that Pete Townshend's run out of ideas, he comes back with a new project so huge, so immense, that you automatically feel ashamed for ever doubting him in the first place. *Bible (Part One)* is such a project, and without a doubt it's the most ambitious thing that The Who have ever chosen to undertake.

Townshend claims that *Part One* alone took him over 35 minutes to write, and the high quality of work present here bears him out. Based on "the world's greatest selling book" (as the ads say), *Bible One* is the first part of a projected series that will be released over the next eighteen months, finally consisting of fifteen parts with ten records per part. Packaged in a huge white box (each part will have a different color to it, so that when all fifteen parts are placed side by side they will form a color scale), *Part One* comes with ten records, a song sheet, and limited edition 125-page color booklet. The whole thing weighs just over 8½ pounds and retails at $24.59, but make no mistake—it's an investment well worth it.

Bible One covers the creation of the world from Genesis to Deuteronomy, with future parts to include Psalms, Proverbs, Jonah, and, of course ("the climax of the work" as Townshend calls it), The New Testament.

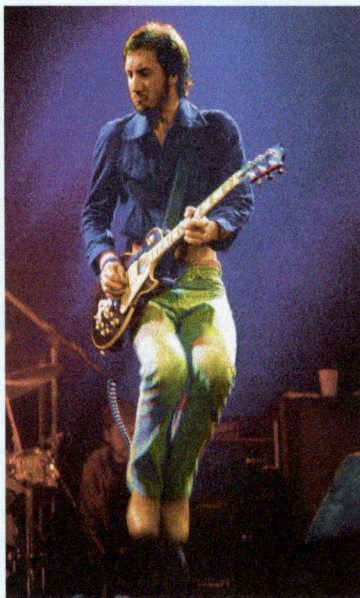

True to fashion, Townshend plays the part of God (in the Introduction to the booklet he says, "I thought the word Narrator would be just a bit too disrespectful . . ."), while Roger, Keith and John take turns at filling out the 132 other roles demanded by *Part One*. The whole series upon completion will require well over 4,000 individual roles to be filled.

Musically, *Part One* suffers most from lack of direction, something that can be observed as its best on sides seven and eight, during the Numbers segment of the work. Townshend seems to be wandering around with his musical ideas, instead of sticking to just one point and seeing it through. Roger Daltrey shines brightest though, especially on side four during the Exodus segment. Under Daltrey's interpretation, Moses never sounded more awe-inspiring. This reviewer personally can't wait to hear Keith Moon's portrayal of Pilate, during Part Thirteen.

In a recent interview, Townshend was asked if he could ever hope to top *Bible*, when it finally gets released in its entirety. He answered that, no, he probably couldn't, and that it would probably be his final work. Knowing Pete, however, I went over to Townshend's house the other day and asked him about the plans for a marathon live concert presentation of *Bible*, for future release as a live album and feature length (*Bible* runs over 80 hours) film. He looked at me, smiled, and I thought I caught a gleam in the corner of his eye.

"Well," he said.
"You never know…"

— CREEM, October 1975

CHAPTER TWO, VERSE 1977
WHO'S KIDDING WHO?

I just received about the fiftieth letter from a Who freak who wants to know when *The Bible* is coming out. It's about time you realized that people actually BELIEVE what they read in that rock 'n' roll rag of yours.

I got a letter from the berk who wrote the piece trying to tell me it was some kind of tribute. Tell him from me if he comes to see me personally some time I'll return the compliment.

In the meantime please print

SOMETHING to let people know that I am not working on a ten album set based on *The Bible*. In fact, I am working on a thirteen album set with Ronnie Lane and Eric Clapton. The story is based on the life of Alexander The Great and his now legendary meeting with Jimmy Carter. The music is going to be recorded in Braille and, dear friends, I know where you live. So please put the record straight otherwise I might try going into competition with you as a journalist.

You wouldn't last a year.
Reflectively yours,
Pete Townshend
Twickenham, England

(It's rough being Jesus in a country with such a shortage of wood, eh? Best that you do go into journalism…maybe you can get a straight answer out of Keith Moon. — Ed.)

— letter to the editor, CREEM, February 1977

CHAPTER THREE, VERSE 2006
THE LAST TESTAMENT

Guarantee: All Pete Townshend Dialogue Is Reported Verbaitsum.

[CHAT ROOM LOG BEGINS]

MODERATOR has entered the room.

PETE TOWNSHEND has entered the room.

MODERATOR: As you all know THE WHO have a new album coming out this month called ENDLESS WIRE and all of us here at Universal Republic Records are

really excited about it!
If you haven't received a review copy yet let me know. I've got a list of all the questions you emailed me and PETE TOWNSHEND is here to answer some of them for you. If there's any time remaining Pete's agreed to answer a few extra ones :) The first question is from Jeffrey Morgan of Creem Magazine who wants to know when "Bible One" is going to come out.

PETE TOWNSHEND: As he well knows this was a gag, and not one

started by me. It was started by someone who thought I was too big for my boots writing rock 'operas' and I needed to be brought down a peg. Oh, how I smarted.

PETE TOWNSHEND has left the room.

MODERATOR: Pete?

[CHAT ROOM LOG ENDS]

— previously unpublished, 2006

**ALICE
COOPER**

SELF SERVING

BOB DYLAN
Slow Train Coming
(Columbia)

FADE IN.

JOHNNY CARSON: My next guest is probably best known for his songs of protest in the mid-Sixties. Since then, he's had a book published, appeared in a movie, and made one of his own. His latest album, *Slow Train Coming*, has just been released, and he's here tonight to talk about it. Would you please welcome *Bob Dylan*.

[*Dylan walks on stage and lip-synchs "Gotta Serve Somebody" to polite applause. He then sits down next to Carson, alongside Robin Williams and Robert Blake.*]

BOB DYLAN: Hi John.

CARSON: Hi Bob. It's great to finally have you on the show.

DYLAN: Uh, well, it's great to finally *be* on the show. [*grins*]

CARSON: What's all this I hear about you becoming a born again Christian? Your new album seems to be pretty heavy.

DYLAN: *Heavy*? Now what do you mean by *heavy*?

CARSON: I don't know. [*laughs and adjusts his tie*] You tell *me*. [*audience laughter*]

DYLAN: Uh, maybe we'd better go on to the next question.

CARSON: You don't want to talk about it?

DYLAN: [*to Williams*] Hey, you're a pretty funny guy.

ROBIN WILLIAMS: Thanks. So are you. Say, you've got little snakes coming out of your hair. Mmmmmm, bad sign.

DYLAN: What?

CARSON: Uh, Bob? Bob? [*audience laughter*] Y'know, I listened to *Slow Train Coming* and I didn't think there was one song on it that matched the religious intensity of "I Dreamed I Saw St. Augustine" or

even "Knocking On Heaven's Door."

DYLAN: That's what *you* say.

ROBERT BLAKE: Baloney, man. You're just scammin'.

DYLAN: What?

BLAKE: *I* listened to that album, man, and I wouldn't let my *dog* toilet train on it. You're *Bob Dylan*, man. What're you wasting your time doin' crap like *that* for? [*audience applause*]

DYLAN: [*to Carson*] Who *is* this guy?

CARSON: Don't mind Robert, he gets a little emotional at times.

BLAKE: Don't give me none of that, John. You *know* it don't got nothin' to do with gospel or religion—and it *certainly* don't got nothin' to do with rock 'n' roll. Leon Russell rocks better than you, man. And at least George Harrison puts up money for Monty Python movies, bottom line. But *you*, man, you're just a *drag*. [*audience applause*] And *that's* the name of *that* tune.

DYLAN: I don't *believe* you.

BLAKE: And I bet you've never worn a *dress*, either.

WILLIAMS: Hey, this is getting interesting.

CARSON: I understand that you're going to do another song for us—

DYLAN: Well, I don't know—

CARSON: Great, we'll—what's that? We do? Listen Bob, we've got to take a small break. Can we do this first?

[*Carson brings out a tin can from beneath his desk*] Is your dog getting it regularly? [*audience laughter*] If not, here's Ed with some tips from new, improved Alpo.

DYLAN: [*pulling out a gun*] HOLD IT! You can't pre-empt me for some *dog food*.

BLAKE: You're *nuts*, man.

WILLIAMS: Mmmmmm, heavy scene.

DYLAN: You don't know what it's *like* to go from selling over two million albums to just a couple of hundred thousand. You think I *wanted* to use Dire Straits on my album? I *had* to. Had to do *something*…

CARSON: You wanna give me the gun now, Bob?

DYLAN: *He* told me what to do. *He* knew that—

ANNOUNCER: We interrupt this program to bring you a special NBC News Report.

CHANCELLOR: Good evening, I'm John Chancellor. At this hour, Bob Dylan, who is probably best known for his songs of protest in the mid-Sixties, is holding the cast, crew, and audience of *The Tonight Show* hostage in NBC's studio 6B.

An agent for the aging folk singer has released a list of Dylan's demands, which reads as follows: First, Dylan demands that his new album sell at least as many copies as the first Boston album did. Second, Dylan demands that his entire back catalog be certified double platinum. Third, Dylan demands that *PTL Club* host Jim Bakker officially replace Johnny Carson as the host of *The Tonight Show*. And fourth, Dylan demands the immediate acquittal and release of Hurricane Carter.

Unless these demands are met within twenty-four hours, Dylan says he will start converting members of the audience to Christianity, one at a time. We'll have more on this story as it happens. We now return you to our regularly scheduled program, which is joined already in progress.

FADE OUT.

— CREEM, December 1979

What do you call a rock star who, at the peak of his arena-packing prowess, allows himself to be subjected to a multiple page written questionnaire; a Rorschach inkblot test; and a tape recorded interview—while being photographed? You call him one helluva good sport, that's what.

MATCH WITS WITH GARY NUMAN!

...if you were him, what would you do?

INTRODUCTION: THE SUBJECT AND THE OBJECT

The way I see it, when you're dealing with these pasty-faced squirts who wanna be synthetic suppositories, y'gotta fight fire with fire—or ice with ice, as the case may be.

I mean, it's no big deal if y'wanna be a machine: be my guest. Just make sure you don't blow your cover by looking back over your shoulder for an audience reaction once you've claimed to've gone and pulled the plug on humanity.

Of course, they always do (pull the plug and look back, that is)—which is one of the reasons I decided to find out, once and for all, if these fly-boys can really take the freezer treatment as well as they like to think they can dish it out.

And what better Subject to subject the rigors of cross-examination to than none other than the guy voted by the populace of Great Britain as being the most like to recede, Mr. Gary Numan.

☆☆☆

The following Case Study is divided into three distinct sections, the first two of which were specifically structured to allow you, the reader, a chance to actively participate in the proceedings.

Section One consist of a 10 question examination. It took The Subject approximately 15 minutes to provide, to the best of his ability, the necessary answers. A similar completion time is recommended for those readers who wish to try their hand at second-guessing how The Subject answered the queries posed to him. (It must be noted that the object of the exercise is *not* to answer how you yourself feel but, rather, how you think The Subject himself responded at the time.)

Section Two consist of six inkblots (reproduced here). The Subject spent between 5 to 15 seconds registering his initial impression to each inkblot. What do you think The Subject saw? Don't forget that imagination is a vital key to this particular section.

Section Three consists of an exclusive interview with The Subject on the eve of his second and (or so he claims) final tour.

Following the interview, The Subject's answers to Sections One and Two will be printed, as well as a brief analysis.

So sharpen your pencils and get ready to match wits with Gary Numan, if you've half a mind.

Remember: He may be richer, but you might be smarter!

☆☆☆
SECTION ONE: THE QUESTIONNAIRE
(Suggested completion time: 15 minutes.)

(1) Given the choice, which of the following two titles would you choose as an album title, and why?
a) Synthecide; b) Neuromantics

(2) List which of your album covers you like, in descending order, and briefly explain why.

(3) Of the following, which mode of transportation do you prefer the most, and why?
a) Airplane; b) Automobile; c) Train; d) Boat

(4) Which of the following forms of entrainment do you favor the most, and why?
a) Television; b) Cinema; c) Records;
d) Literature

(5) Name your favorite:
a) Movie Director; b) Actor/Actress;
c) Author; d) Musician; e) Artist

(6) What do you fear the most, and why?

(7) Describe briefly the happiest day of your life.

(8) Do you dream in color or black and white? Also, describe the one dream or nightmare you can remember the most vividly.

(9) Name one way in which your success has changed you for the better. Name one way in which your success has changed you for the worst.

(10) Are you happy?

☆☆☆
SECTION TWO: THE RORSCHACH TEST
(Suggested reaction time: between 5 and 15 seconds per inkblot.)

☆☆☆
SECTION THREE: THE INTERVIEW

OBSERVER: Is Numan your real name?
SUBJECT: No, my real name is Webb.

☆☆☆

OBSERVER: Do you have your pilot's license yet?
SUBJECT: No, I'm getting it at Christmas. I've done the flying, but I still have to do the written exams.
OBSERVER: Did you pass the flying test?
SUBJECT: Yes, there's two. There's a general flight test, which includes actual handling of the aircraft and procedures, and there's a cross-country.
OBSERVER: Does the written test involve a lot of studying?
SUBJECT: A fair bit. It all depends on how clever you are. If you're really bright you can do it fairly quickly. If you're not so bright, you have to study.
OBSERVER: Do you have to study?
SUBJECT: I'm alright, actually. Most of the questions are multiple choice. There's not that much pressure.
OBSERVER: What does flying have that rock 'n' roll doesn't?
SUBJECT: It doesn't have people telling you that you're shit. And that's all. It has everything else that rock 'n' roll's got. It's very satisfying to do it. It has the ego, in one way, because, as you get out in an airplane, you feel very proud—even if no one's there. It has a far

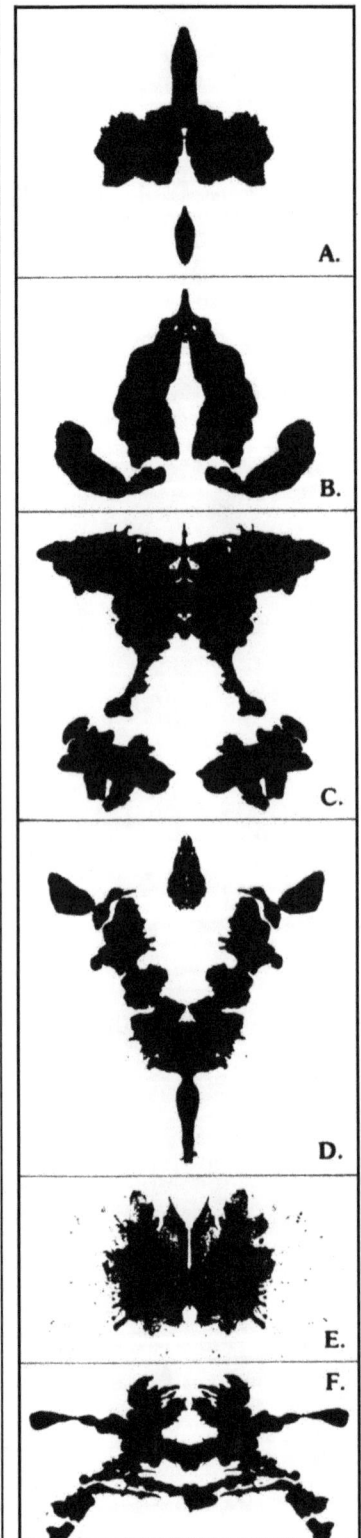

A.

B.

C.

D.

E.

F.

Photos: ©Tom Robe

more personal thing in an airplane. And in that way, I think it's better than rock 'n' roll. It has all the excitement and, to an extent, the glamour.

☆☆☆

OBSERVER: Is this your last tour?

SUBJECT: The *Telekon* tour is the last tour. There'll be at least two more albums, at least, of new material—and I also want to put out a double live, too. After that, I've no plans to make another one, but if I'm still writing songs, I will. It's no big thing that I'm going to stop because I enjoy doing it.

OBSERVER: Just how calculated has this whole thing been?

SUBJECT: It was totally premeditated. It was a complete plan. A strategy...well, it's about a year or two years ahead of schedule because it all happened far quicker than I thought it would. But once it *did* happen quickly, we just moved the plan two years ahead and skipped the bit in between. We're still following the plan now, practically to the week. Virtually.

We worked out the plan almost exactly to within two or three months: "Round about September, October we'll be doing this in *that* year, and that will follow onto this in *that* year..." So we've had to revise it and alter it slightly as things have happened quicker or slower in certain territories. And because it's around the world, other territories were slower to catch on, so we've had to revise the plan in certain areas. But, basically, it's still going exactly as it should be.

OBSERVER: When you say that this is the last tour, do you really not need it enough that you'll stick by your guns and not be back on the boards in another eighteen months?

SUBJECT: I don't need it at all. I certainly don't need to keep touring. I don't need it to make money 'cause I lose a fortune touring. I don't think I need it to sell records, certainly not.

I wouldn't want to be in a position where I'm selling the most records all the time, because that you have to keep doing to save face. I'd rather reach a lower level where there's no big pressure to keep getting number ones, but it's also enough to keep you within the top half a dozen people. To be number six is fine. It's the best place to be in terms of records, actually.

☆☆☆

OBSERVER: Do you like Bach?

SUBJECT: Who?

OBSERVER: Bach. You know, the composer.

SUBJECT: Oh yeah. Some of it.

OBSERVER: The cello suites?

SUBJECT: Yeah. I used to have a teacher who played the cello.

☆☆☆

OBSERVER: Do you plan on settling down and having children?

SUBJECT: Yeah, I'm going to get married.

OBSERVER: Have you found the girl yet?

SUBJECT: Could be.

☆☆☆

OBSERVER: Why do you tour with your parents?

SUBJECT: I think it's got a big taboo. People are very embarrassed to go around with their parents—and for that reason they don't take them: because they feel embarrassed by it.

I bring them because, obviously, the first thing is that they work, so I wouldn't be without them for that reason. I also wouldn't want to be without them because I wouldn't want to leave them for that length of time. They help me keep my feet on the ground and not get "star trip" problems, and it's just nice to have them around. I just like them being there. Someone to talk to if things don't go quite right.

☆☆☆

OBSERVER: Is there anything else you would like to talk about? Perhaps the usual stuff: you know, paranoia...

SUBJECT: No! I *always* talk about that, it's *boring*. I'm not paranoid...

☆☆☆

APPENDIX 1:
GARY NUMAN'S QUESTIONNAIRE RESPONSES

(1) *Neuromantics*. It sounds better and the other is suicide or as good as, and I'm no longer interest in such gloomy subjects.

(2): *Telekon*. Probably because it's new and I'm not tired of it yet.

Replicas. It fits the music. It's actually what I pictured as I wrote then album.

Tubeway Army. My best friend did the drawing. It's simple, but most effective.

The Pleasure Principle. Nice parody, but no one realized. [*Jeffrey Morgan realized: The front and back covers of* The Pleasure Principle *are a parody of the front and back inner sleeve photos of* Sound-On-Sound *by Bill Nelson's Red Noise*.]

(3) Airplane. Only as a pilot. Incredibly satisfying.

(4) Television. I don't have to go out. It encompasses the others to some degree. It's the most varied...

(5) a) Spielberg; b) Clint Eastwood / [*left blank*]; c) Tolkien; d) [*left blank*]; e) Magritte.

(6) Losing a limb / Vanity.

(7) I haven't had it yet.

(8) Both. (In black & white:) Skiing along a grey corridor on two water pipes, and eventually pricking my finger, whereupon it split into two with three connecting tubes. Then I woke up.

(9) I'm happier. I'm very agitated.

(10) Yes, at times. Who isn't at times?

☆☆☆

APPENDIX 2:
GARY NUMAN'S RORSCHACH RESPONSES

A: It's a missile taking off.

B: Clown's feet.

C: It's a butterfly with a swan's head.

D: [*laughs*] God knows. Looks like it's got a, like a *rat's* head up on that top little bit [*points*] and a cow's ears—like a cow's skull and like it's on a stand...like a lampshade.

E: A butterfly being shot to bits.

F: Crab.

☆☆☆

CONCLUSION:
IS GARY HUMAN?

Hey, c'mon, are you *kidding* me? You *betcha* he's human—just ask him about Miss Pinky from Montreal the next time you see him and you'll find out how human he really *is*.

Meanwhile, the test results speak or themselves...and y'know what? I kinda *expected* them to. Y'see, I got this theory that the only *real* robots in this business are Kraftwerk's Ralf and Florian—but even there I'm probably far off the mark, right?

Or *am* I?

☆☆☆

"We have cassette recorders built into our heads. This is called tape consciousness. It is the invention of Telefunken-Magnetophone here in Germany. Since the day they invented the tape recorder there has developed not only a new hardware of machine, but also a new software of people. We think that the two must be synchronized. We play the machine, but the machines also play us." — Ralf Hutter, 1977

"The whole world is becoming humanoid! People who *look* like humans, but are *not!*" — Howard Beale, 1976

— CREEM, January 1981

JEFFREY MORGAN

To quote Norman Mailer on the fine art of concocted conversation: "Not literally true, but aesthetically true."

TOUGH GUYS DON'T NANCE

SOMEWHERE OUT IN THE PACIFIC – In a surprise move that has some legal observers shaking their heads in wonder and others asking why it took so long to happen, former Rolling Stones manager Allen Klein has filed a copyright infringement lawsuit against veteran rocker Neil Young over a song that appears on Young's 1975 album *Tonight's The Night*. In it, Klein alleges that the song in question, "Borrowed Tune," uses the exact same music and vocal melody as The Rolling Stones' 1966 single "Lady Jane."

"Alleges my ass!" Klein roars as he smokes a Panatela on the upper deck of his spacious yacht *The Bastard*, which also serves as a floating ABKCO Industries World Headquarters. "Everybody knows this is nowhere *close* to being debatable. The song's called 'Borrowed Tune' ferkeefssake and Neil even *admits* as much when he whines: 'I'm singing this borrowed tune I took from The Rolling Stones'! What *more* proof do you need? It's an open and shut case, just like when I sued Joe Cocker for illegally writing those unintelligible new lyrics to 'Honky Tonk Women' on *Mad Dogs & Englishmen*. Did you ever hear his rewritten version of 'The Under Assistant West Coast Promotion Man'? Just horrible. I had to put a stop to it."

Mention that it's taken over thirty years for him to file the lawsuit, and Klein merely shrugs. "I've been *busy*. Managing The Beatles. Managing the Stones. Getting the Stones' entire back catalogue from Decca. Remastering all of the albums. Re-releasing them on ABKCO. Cashing the checks. Counting the money. This is the first free time I've had in *years*. Besides," Klein laughs, "I figured that the longer I waited, the more records Neil might sell."

Which brings up the matter of how much compensation Klein is seeking. "Well, obviously that depends on how many copies of *Tonight's The Night* have been sold since 1975. Unfortunately we're not talking about *Harvest* here, we're talking about the most depressing album ever recorded in the entire history of the human eardrum. Worse than *Berlin*. But once we get a look at the latest sales figures—which I hear are barely a few thousand, if that—we'll be able to make an honest determination of what's fair,

even if it means only getting a little gelt out of the deal. It's the principle of the thing."

Klein pauses to light another cigar. "Don't get me wrong. I'm a big Neil Young fan. I love *Arc*. But if I don't make an example out of him, where will it end? What if Crosby, Stills and Nash decide to change 'Sing This All Together (See What Happens)' without permission? As a businessman I have a fiduciary obligation to Betty and myself to make sure that this kind of thing never occurs again—and I assure you it won't. At ABKCO, the buck stops here."

Asked if there's any truth to the rumor that his next business move will be to file a libel suit against writer and producer Eric Idle for the former Python's less than flattering portrayal of Klein as Ron Decline in the 1978 movie *The Rutles: All You Need Is Cash*, the most feared manager in the world slowly takes the cigar out of his mouth and smiles.

"I'm in no hurry," Allen Klein says, gently tapping a thick roll of ash loose. "Time is on my side."

— CREEM, December 2007

Neil Young & Crazy Horse - Photo Credit © Robert Matheu

CAREER ADVICE FROM ALICE COOPER

My favorite night at Toronto's legendary Massey Hall was on the evening of November 30th 1974 when Northern Secondary High School put on its third annual musical showcase. Like the two before it, "SCANORAMA '74" was the brainchild of Northern's two music department directors, Bill and Evelyn Tummon, and was used as a school fundraiser.

No slouches when it came to treading the boards, the two had already produced a number of successful school auditorium revues, such as "SHOWCASE OF SHOWS" which, according to the one dollar ducat, was nothing less than "Northern's 250 voice choir's version of THE BEST OF BROADWAY" and featured excerpts from such classic musicals as *Porgy And*

Bess, Showboat, Annie Get Your Gun, West Side Story, South Pacific, Bye Bye Birdie, Fiddler On The Roof, and *Camelot*.

However, the evening's entertainment at Massey Hall this night in 1974 started on a decidedly more contemporary note. Opening the show, standing on a riser high above the choir, was Northern Secondary's very own twenty-year-old Student Council President. Rakishly resplendent in sequined top hat and tails; knee-high boots; white kid gloves; and brandishing a cane, he began the proceedings by singing "Hello Hooray" to a solo piano accompaniment. As it happened, the moment was fortuitously forever preserved for posterity by a classmate's uncle who happened to be in the audience with a camera.

Forty years later, I presented Alice with an autographed 8x10 glossy of that performance, signed: "Coop: Thanks for the inspiration in 1974."

Upon seeing the photograph, Alice laughed and said: "Oh, that's great! That's going in the archive!" Then, pausing to study the image further, he added: "That's your look. You should go with that."

I began to demur, but Alice interrupted me. "No," he said seriously, "you should continue doing that. Once you have the talent, you never lose it."

— previously unpublished, 2021

DAVID BOWIE

ROBERTA FLACK

JOYCE KENNEDY

MACEO PARKER

ELLIOTT MURPHY'S FICTIONALIZED HISTORY

He has had four albums released: *Aquashow, Lost Generation, Night Lights* and *Just A Story From America*. His articles and interviews have appeared in various magazines including *Rolling Stone* and *Circus*. He wrote the liner notes for the Velvet Underground's live *1969* album. His name is Elliott Murphy. He is a writer.

JEFFREY MORGAN: There's a line in "Hollywood" that goes: "Hollywood, you've shaped my life like a Technicolor carving knife" and another one in "Deco Dance" that "the past is the only thing that survives." Somewhere between those two lines is a summation of what you're all about. I don't see your albums as individual albums as much as I see them as different acts in one giant play

wherein different characters from history and popular culture wander in and make cameos. There's hardly anybody you haven't mentioned: F. Scott Fitzgerald, Brian Jones, Patti Smith, Isadora Duncan—

ELLIOTT MURPHY: I've got to write some more about Brian Jones. I'm not through with him yet. I believe in fictionalized history. Rock 'n' roll should tell history, too.

MORGAN: In your songs you don't seem to want to let people forget. You always keep on bringing up the past and putting it in front of your listeners.

MURPHY: That's real interesting; that's real true. I've never thought about that.

MORGAN: You're a fan and you don't try

to hide it, do you?

MURPHY: Yeah, I'm a real fan. I consider myself a third generation—I mean, if you consider the first generation were people like Chuck Berry and Elvis Presley and the second generation was The Beatles and Rolling Stones and Dylan, then I'm definitely third generation and I never think that I'm in competition with that second generation. I'm not ashamed to say that I'm really influenced by them.

I believe in historical rock. See, I mean, someone like Brian Jones: if rock 'n' roll people don't write songs about Brian Jones and sing about Brian Jones, how is anyone going to remember him? I've talked to sixteen-year-old kids and asked them who Brian Jones was and *they don't know.* But they know who the Rolling Stones are. So maybe it's my duty. I always write about the same thing. I mean, any good author really writes about the same thing. It's like fatalistic romanticism: you know there's not going to be a happy ending but you keep hoping for it.

MORGAN: Around the time of *Lost Generation* you wrote a biography where you said that you worked as an extra in Fellini's *Roma.* How did that come about?

MURPHY: As soon as I got out of school, when I was seventeen, I started traveling. I lived in Key West, Florida for a while 'cause I always liked these authors and I always wanted to go where they went. That's where Hemingway used to live. Then I went over to Europe with just a couple of hundred dollars and I ran out of money very quickly.

Luckily, I found this agent for movie actors and I told him that I could ride horses. I told him that I was a cowboy actor; that I'd been in *Rawhide* for years and years as an extra. At the time they were making all of those spaghetti westerns but he said that they weren't making any Clint Eastwood westerns then; the only thing they were doing was Fellini, so I was taken out to do an interview with him. They stuck me in a room and Fellini opened the door about an inch and just looked in for about ten minutes. Just so I could see his face and know he was looking. He just had me sit there in his office and squirm like I was under a microscope—he never came into the room, never said anything—and that's how I got the job. I was hired as an extra, which is how he hires everyone.

After the film, however, I decided that I didn't want to be an actor. I had a couple of other films lined up 'cause I had blond hair and they were making all these Nazi movies at the time like *The Damned* and *The Conformist.* They wanted me to get my hair cut, though, and I wouldn't do it. Besides, after one film I was already fed up with the whole movie industry so I came back to the States for a little while.

MORGAN: How did you end up doing the liner notes for the Velvet Underground's *1969* album?

MURPHY: Well, Paul Nelson, who was working at Mercury, was really the guy who discovered me at the Mercer Arts Center. He asked me to do it and I did 'cause I'd always been a Velvet Underground fan.

MORGAN: So *that's* how you got in *Circus* doing the interview with Lou Reed about *Metal Machine*—

MURPHY: Yeah! No, by that time I had become friends with Lou—which was probably my biggest mistake. I'd met Lou for a few times in New York but never

really knew him. Then one day my Mother called me up and she said: "This young man just called here looking for you. Really nice young gentleman named Louis Reed and I talked to him for about half an hour. He left this number for you to call."

Lou can really be a great guy. To call Lou Reed a great guy just sounds crazy, but he can be very normal. He grew up a mile from where I grew up. He's from Freeport, Long Island and I'm from Garden City, so we sort of come from the same place—not mentally. I don't think Lou's seen daylight in years. Lou has great theories, though. Like how polluted air is really good for you; that his body had adapted itself to it.

MORGAN: The way I understood it, Lou was going to produce your third album. What happened?

MURPHY: We were going to do it in the RCA studios up here with Lou, but then Lou got a little crazy. He got more involved with *Sally Can't Dance* and I really wanted a change of weather so I went out to California. Another big influence on me has always been The Doors. Jim Morrison I think is one of the only real poets in rock 'n' roll.

MORGAN: With all of your influences, do you ever wonder who Elliott Murphy really is? Do you ever look into a mirror and see a central core there?

MURPHY: My whole life I've always been shocked when I look into a mirror, it's an odd— I think, maybe, if anything, I'm a journalistic rock 'n' roller.

MORGAN: Still searching yourself out?

MURPHY: Still searching.

— **previously unpublished, 1977**

WITH MY HEART ON MY SLEEVE)
Elliott Murphy

THE WHO

A ROCK STAR'S GUIDE TO ROCK PHOTOGRAPHY

LESSON 21: THE INADVERTENT INDIFFERENT IMAGE

The rock star should never pose for a photograph without first checking to see if anyone else is in the vicinity, loitering without intent. Failure to do so may risk exposing the rock star to ridicule because he didn't know that there was a rock critic perched on an equipment trunk behind him, terminally bored out of his ever-lovin' blue-eyed mind.

**FREDDIE
MERCURY
AND
BRIAN MAY**

The conversation you are about to read is true. The name of the Toronto hotel restaurant has been omitted to protect the establishment.

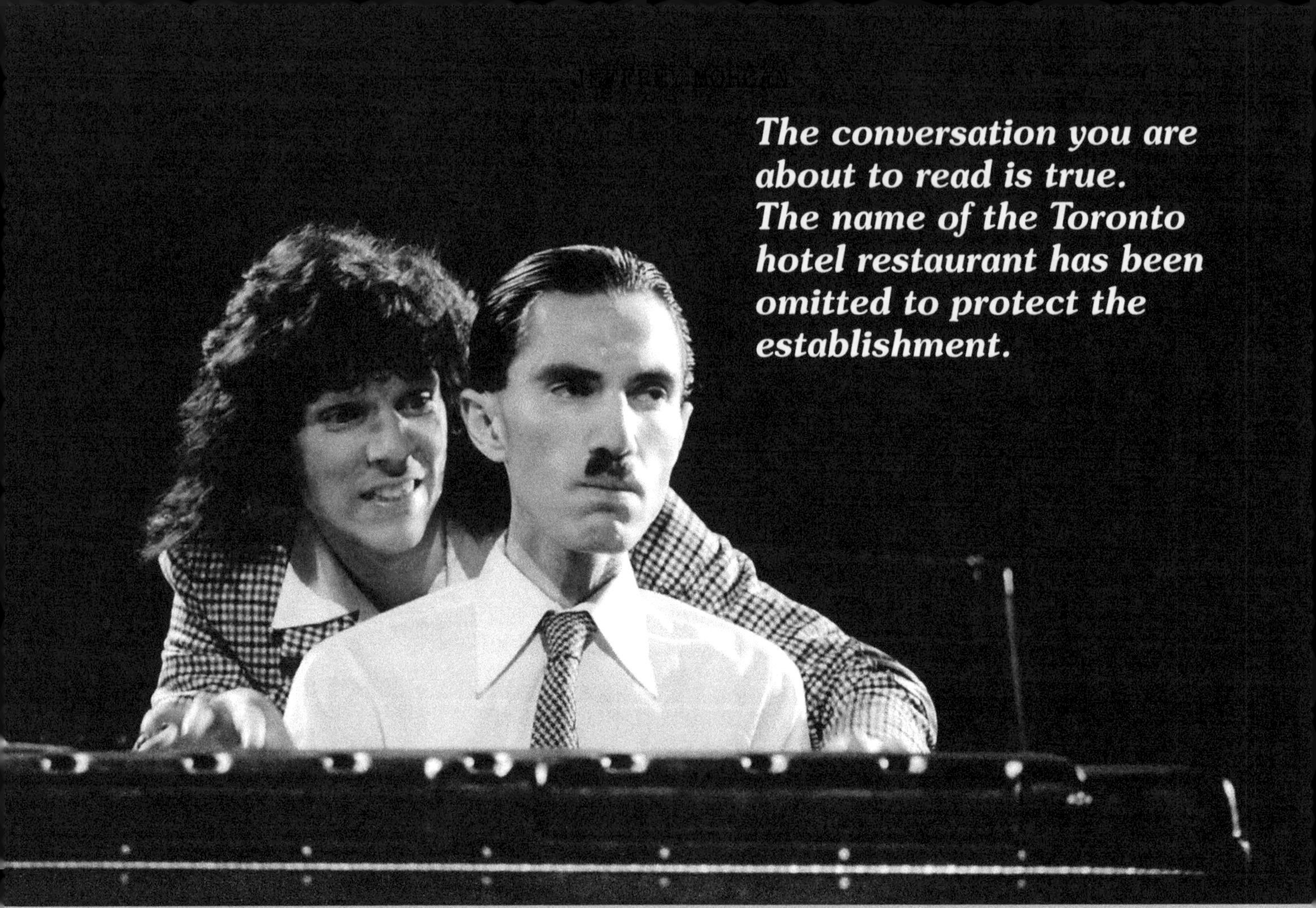

WAITRESS AND APOLOGIES MY BREAKFAST WITH SPARKS

JEFFREY MORGAN: Have you abandoned your photography career?

RON MAEL: No, actually, I just took a bunch… I'm now… I've abandoned my Canon and I bought a three pound Polaroid black and white camera and I'm doing a book on chambermaids in Europe, and I took—

RUSSELL MAEL: It's finished.

RON: What?

RUSSELL: It's finished.

RON: Oh, it's finished, yeah.

MORGAN: It sounds like a David Hamilton book.

RON: Yeah, it's sorta that…

MORGAN: I see color transparencies of these chambermaids with soft light coming through the windows…

RON: This ain't got no soft light 'cause it's a Polaroid. Cold facts.

RUSSELL: It's only got available light.

RON: [laughing] Not even much of that.

MORGAN: Is this going to be one of those small little books that you get in the art shops, or is this—

RON: Yeah, it's an art shop book, like *Aperture Magazine* or something.

MORGAN: *Focal Length*…

RON: Yeah.

MORGAN: Will it be available widely or is it going to be—

RON: I hope so, yeah. It's from all the cities we've played before coming to the States. Helsinki…

MORGAN: Dare I ask: Why chambermaids?

RON: Well, it's something we run into all the time, and they're all kinda the same and it was an easy thing for me to do because we're in so many hotels in so many cities that they're always there every morning.

RUSSELL: *[to the waitress]* Can I get some milk please for the tea? Please?

MORGAN: I see that you're not bothering your brother too much on stage these days.

RUSSELL: Yeah, I'm laying off him a bit.

MORGAN: As he writes more complicated piano parts he's got to concentrate—

RUSSELL: Yeah…

RON: Yeah!

RUSSELL: I gotta sing better. I wanna be another singer…

MORGAN: Another Sinatra.

RUSSELL: Yeah…

RON: Oh, boy, is this a… I actually wanted plain yogurt. These look like flavored.

WAITRESS: *[bringing milk and yogurt]* They are.

RON: Well, I'm sure she's got plain yogurt.

WAITRESS: Just flavored. If you don't want it, it's all right. But that's all we have, sorry.

RUSSELL: You didn't have any choice of which flavor you could get.

RON: Yeah.

RUSSELL: Boy…

WAITRESS: They're the last two left. *[she leaves]*

RUSSELL: Oh, I see.

RON: The last two left from last night. *Boy*, I don't like this place.

MORGAN: There's a nice view.

RON: Yeah. Too bad my back is to it.

RUSSELL: This tastes like fruit yogurt. The menu said plain yogurt.

RON: I know.

RUSSELL: That's what I wanted. Plain yogurt.

RON: And they tell you that's all they've got, and it's obviously been prepared. *[laughs]* It's really weird. I'm going to send it back.

RUSSELL: I'm going to send it back after eating it…

RON: Yeah.

MORGAN: You didn't do "Pineapple."

RUSSELL: No, we just didn't work it out this tour but next time… Next time you see us we may do it.

MORGAN: Are you being squeezed out

of the writing chores?

RUSSELL: Oh, I'm not being squeezed out—

RON: He's phasing himself out. *[laughs]*

MORGAN: You're phasing yourself out?

RUSSELL: Yeah, it's a—

RON: It's self-imposed sqeezedom. *[more food is brought to the table]*

RUSSELL: Thanks.

RON: A buttered bagel! Sacrilege! [laughs]

RUSSELL: Ah, dear boy. You can't get good help these days. They butter your bagel, they give you Strawberry yogurt when you said plain—

RON: I ask you… I ask you…

RUSSELL: —they give you four Kadota figs—

RON: *[taking one]* Three now. *[laughter]*

RUSSELL: Have a Kadota fig before they're all gone. What flavor is your yogurt?

RON: I really haven't figured it out yet. I think it's vanilla.

RUSSELL: That's better than mine.

Would you like a Kadota fig?

MORGAN: No, thank you.

RON: Want a Kadota fig for the top of your pancakes?

MORGAN: It *would* look nice, but I'm afraid that I didn't bring my camera.

RUSSELL: Can I try a spoon of this?

RON: Yeah, you can have the rest.

RUSSELL: I don't want to mix it with my other flavor. I'll just put it down here.

RON: What's that other flavor? Concord grape or something?

RUSSELL: It's real boring… Concord raspberry or something.

MORGAN: Oh, what happened last night when that girl jumped on stage?

RON: Some girl just jumped on stage and grabbed me and gave me a… A hot juicy one, as they say.

RUSSELL: *[laughing]* A hot juicy one!

RON: She picked a really funny moment 'cause that's the tender part, the start of "Never Turn Your Back On Mother Earth" where, y'know, sunrise and all

that, and she just jumped on stage and grabbed me around the neck and said "I love you," and then she said—

RUSSELL: "Gotta go now!" *[laughter]*

RON: No…

RUSSELL: "Gotta run!" *[more laughter]*

RON: No, she didn't say that, she said: "I think I'll wait until the light comes on." Then she just jumped off. She really was aware of being on stage.

RUSSELL: The last time that happened, it happened in the middle of that same song once in England. Kids know that the lights are gonna dim in that song and so if anybody has any thoughts of getting on board, they just…

RON: The coast is clear.

RUSSELL: Yeah, that's the one when the getting's good, is that song.

RON: It really took me by surprise because that sort of thing happens in England, but usually doesn't tend to happen here.

MORGAN: How much do you get mobbed?

RUSSELL: There's a twenty-five minute film that was shot during the last English concert we had, and by the end of the film, I'm like…pinned to the floor underneath about ten girls and it's really an amazing thing. It was in the encore that it happened. It's really a fun film.

MORGAN: It may be a fun film, but what were you thinking while you were being pinned by these ten girls?

RUSSELL: Oh, it's fun; it reminded me of when I played football in high school. You know; things like the pile-up—

MORGAN: Only *they* were softer.

RUSSELL: Yeah. *[laughter]* That's it.

RON: Some of them were bigger though… *[more laughter]*

MORGAN: What I'm most impressed by is the humor in your lyrics and the fact that your songwriting is the most satirically literate in the whole business—something that's sorely needed these days.

RON: They always seem to ask me: "What's the future of rock and all?" And it's not going to be that it's this big change or anything like that. It's just the fact that if all goes well there'll be more people that are into writing things that do have some sort of personalized point of view, and that they can put them down into some sort of musical context.

The other thing along those lines is what's happened a lot—particularly in England—is that the visuals have tended to cover the fact that there are songs there. And so, in a way, people are seeing it the reverse of how you're seeing it. I'd prefer to see it your way, and that seems to be the proper emphasis.

RUSSELL: Our image has gotten bigger than what's really there—than the substance behind it—so a lot of people think automatically when you say "Sparks"... "Oh, it's the two guys that one's so different from the other one" and that sort of thing. And we like to think of it like *you* did; that there's—

RON: Substance there.

RUSSELL: Yeah, yeah. *[looking down at his plate]* It looks like I haven't even—

RON: Begun.

RUSSELL: Yeah, I know. It's like a gimmick or something. Like, they've got a banana nut pancake, and they don't have them anymore.

RON: And if you want a large glass of carrot juice, forget it. What they're doing is that they have all this really good menu and then they're taking off all the frilly stuff. I bet you couldn't get that cheese and lobster sandwich.

RUSSELL: Yeah, I'll bet you couldn't.

RON: It's probably cheese and bacon.

RUSSELL: They'll say: "Sorry, lobster's off today, love." *[laughter]*

RON: Cheese and lobster sandwich: Fifteen dollars. They have a melted...a grilled cheese and lobster sandwich.

RUSSELL: They put this whole lobster between two pieces of white bread. *[laughter]*

RON: One and a quarter live main lobster on French roll with garnish. If I hadn't bought an apple from last night..

RUSSELL: I've got a pineapple in my room—

RON: Why don't you bring *that* down?

RUSSELL: I'm going to use it on the plane. Somebody gave me a pineapple, of all things. A great big pineapple. I can't imagine why...

MORGAN: They'll think it's a bomb. They won't let you bring it into the country. They'll think it's tainted or something.

RUSSELL: Oh yeah, it's another country, isn't it?

RON: You'll have to go through customs.

MORGAN: "Pineapple! I wrote a song about it!"

RON: It goes something like this...

MORGAN: "Step over here, sir, please."

RUSSELL: Yeah. *[laughs]*

MORGAN: Have you got a tip to leave the waitress?

RUSSELL: It's a mean cruel sea when it comes to double-crossing time.

MORGAN: Check, please!

— Cheap Thrills, March 1976

Ron Mael & Dick Clark. Photograph: ©Robert Matheu

This was the first article to attain over one million unique hits on the original CREEM website. One of the million who read it was Rolling Stones producer Don Was, who was in Paris recording A Bigger Bang. He showed it to the Stones, who got quite a good laugh out of it—none more so than Keith Richards, who then showed it to Johnny Depp who, ten years later in 2014, told Script Doctor Matheu that he still fondly remembered it as being cool.

WORLD EXCLUSIVE!
KEITH RICHARDS & JOHNNY DEPP HIRE CREEM HACKS!
by The Script Doctors: Matheu & Morgan

Musso & Franks grill on Hollywood Boulevard is the oldest and swankiest place in Hollywood; vintage high back wood booths and tin ceiling tile make it the ideal kind of location that Keith Richards and Johnny Depp would pick for a story conference.

After publicly griping to anyone who would listen that the leaked first draft "wasn't rock 'n' roll enough," we were put on a retainer as script doctors to punch up key sections of the first draft of Disney's forthcoming major motion picture *Pirates Of The Caribbean: Treasures Of The Lost Abyss.*

In it, Johnny Depp will be making his first movie sequel by reprising his Oscar-nominated role as Captain Jack Sparrow, while the real-life inspiration for his character, Rolling Stones guitarist Keith Richards, will be making his acting debut as Jack's estranged father, the notorious pirate Daddy Jack.

With a tape recorder running to capture every comment, we began showing Depp and Richards the revisions we had made. First up was an action scene on page 124 which featured a large battle between Captain Jack's ship and a rival pirate vessel. We explained that the scene needed an additional incident to show Jack's ability to light a fire under his men and motivate them despite the odds being overwhelmingly against them.

To convey this, we had written a new scene just before the fight begins where Captain Jack swings onto the deck with his sword held high, and rouses the gang's spirits by passionately yelling out: "I'll fight but not surrender cried . . . the wild Caribbean boy!"

"I like that!" Johnny said enthusiastically upon hearing it. "It might even become a catchphrase or something! You've got to admit it's got a nice rhythm to it…" At this point, he began humming to himself: *"I'll*

fight but not surrender cried…"

"No, no, no…" Keith muttered, looking over. "I *hate* that line."

"Why?" a perplexed Johnny asked. "What's wrong with it?"

"Deppo, it *reminds* me of something," Keith drawled. "Something unpleasant that I can't put my finger on. And I *especially* don't like this line on the next page where you have me saying: 'Friend or foe, stand and deliver! Your money or your life!' "

We started to speak, but Keith raised a skull-ringed hand to protest. "I'm serious but not desperate," he slurred. "And I *am* adamant."

That's all right, we suggested; we can come back to it later. Next up was a scene on page 168 when Sparrow's gang of pirates starts fighting amongst themselves over a stash of loot while the ship is in port. We'd added a new scene where Jack and his Dad take a stand on the deck and display their strong authority by confronting the rebellious crew.

Looking at the additional passages marked in the script, Johnny and Keith began reading their new dialogue aloud.

CAPT'N JACK: Hey…hey pirates! Come on now! That means everybody just cool out! Will you cool out everybody?

DADDY JACK: A fight broke out.

CAPT'N JACK: I know. I'm hip. Everybody be cool now. Come on, all right? Uh, pirates, I mean, who's fighting what for? Who's fighting and what for? We don't want to fight, come on!

DADDY JACK: [*pointing*] Look, that guy there, if he doesn't stop it, man… Listen, either those cats cool it, man, or we don't sail!

"Wait a minute," Johnny said, shaking his head slowly. "I'm afraid those lines don't sound very believable to me. I honestly can't

imagine anyone saying something as weak and ineffective as that in a life threatening situation."

"Either those cats cool it or we don't sail?" Keith wheezed. "What kind of lame ultimatum is that? This is supposed to be *Pirates Of The Caribbean* not *Pansies Of The Caribbean.*"

Suddenly Keith dropped his script and began laughing out loud. "Now *this* is a new line that I *definitely* like!"

"What line is that?" Johnny asked, looking over.

"Here, on the last page," Keith indicated. "It's the final scene where we've reconciled. You make a sarcastic remark and I turn to you and say: 'Comical little geezer, aren't ya? You'll look funny when you're fifty.' " Once again Keith roared with laughter.

"I don't find that line humorous at all."

"Johnny, Johnny, Johnny," Keith Richards rasped, draping a hand over Depp's shoulder. "You shouldn't take it so hard!"

At this point, with the proceedings declining and the bar tab climbing, we managed to surreptitiously slip out the back door. As we left, the MFIC yelled over his shoulder: "We'll bid you both a fond adieu! On with the show, to Hell with you!"

— CREEM, November 2004

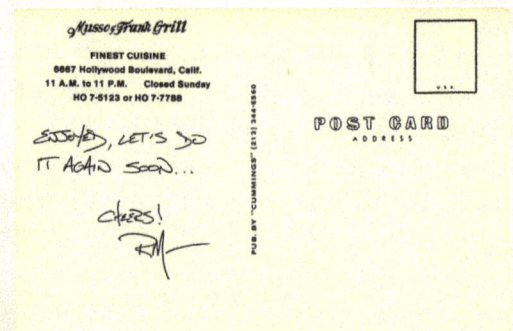

Musso Frank Grill
FINEST CUISINE
6667 Hollywood Boulevard, Calif.
11 A.M. to 11 P.M.   Closed Sunday
HO 7-5123 or HO 7-7788

ENJOYED, LET'S DO
IT AGAIN SOON…

CHEERS!
RM

POST CARD
ADDRESS

THE ROLLING STONES

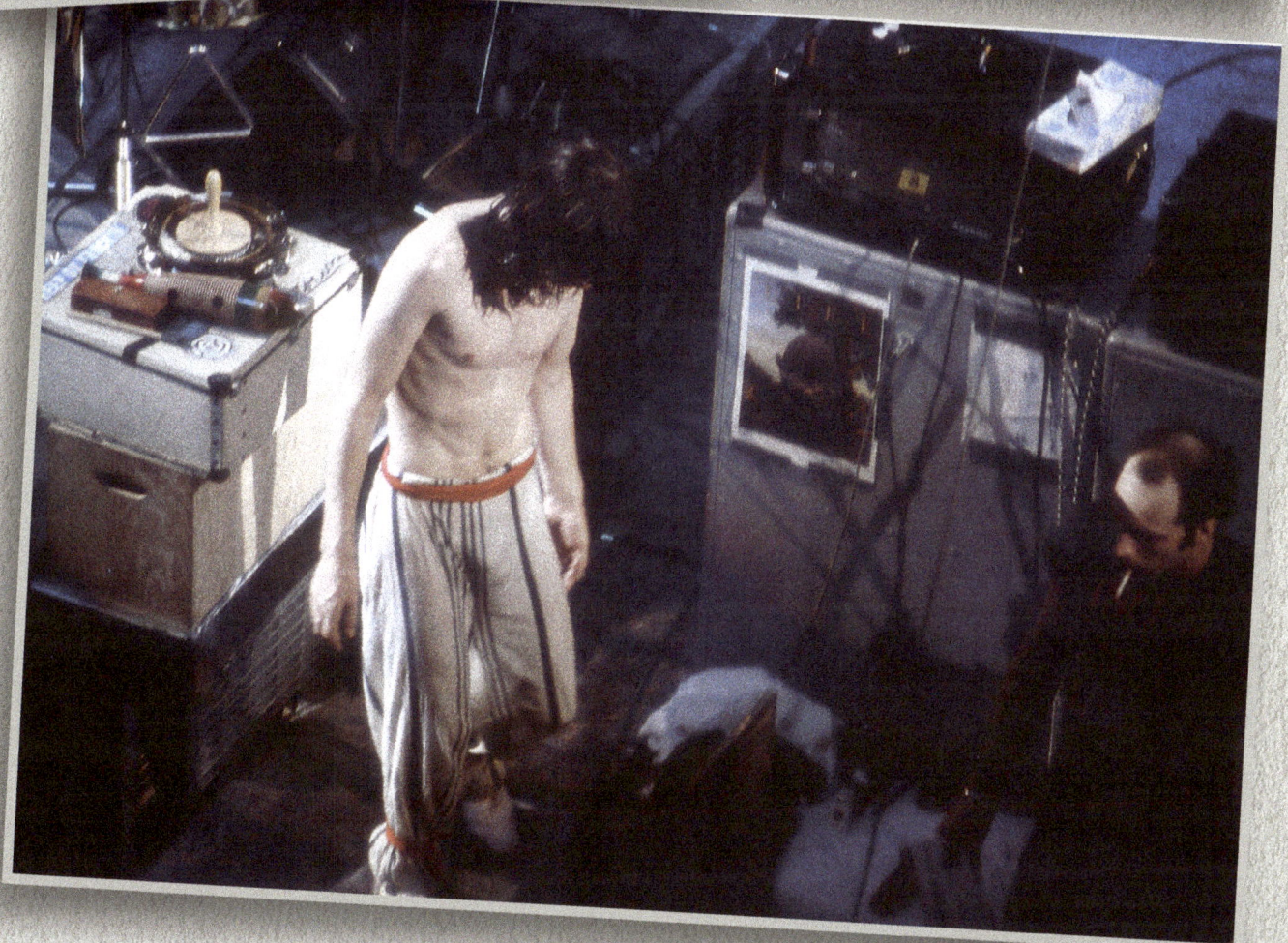

THE DEFINITIVE
LOU REED
INTERVIEW

Soon after I began writing for CREEM, I was hired by Marty Herzog to become the editor of a free monthly small circulation music publication called Cheap Thrills *which, literally, was Canada's Only Rock 'n' Roll Magazine.*

Thus it was for Cheap Thrills that on March 18th 1976, I first interviewed a 34-year-old Lou Reed who had come to Toronto to promote his eighth solo album in four years, Coney Island Baby. *After the release of* Metal Machine Music *a year earlier, RCA felt that Lou had to smooth over that imbroglio by taking the extra step of seriously promoting his new album.*

During the course of our three hour lunch downtown at Trader Vic's in the Hotel Toronto, Lou thoroughly discussed as many aspects of his life and art as time would allow in a sincere, friendly manner.

But because the magazine was restricted in size to a limited number of pages, only an extremely small portion of our lengthy conversation could be printed in Cheap Thrills. *And even then, it had to be spread out as a feature cover story over three consecutive monthly issues.*

In October of 1976, I spoke with Lou briefly for a second time before Rock And Roll Heart *was released. Lou was pleasantly surprised when I presented him with copies of all three installments of our first interview, and he avidly flipped through them prior to the start of our recorded conversation.*

Little did either one of us know that, fifteen years later, I would take a line from "Some Kinda Love" and use it to name Lou's four disc RCA box set: Between Thought And Expression *- a title that Lou liked so much, he also used it for his own lyrical collection. If you have copy of the box set's booklet, you could look it up.*

It has been said that all good things come to those who wait. And so, forty-five years later, here is the definitive Lou Reed interview as it should have appeared back in 1976. Needless to say, I'm extremely gratified that this valuable historical document is finally seeing the light of day in Rock Critic Confidential, *unabridged, as initially intended.*

One final observation: you'll note how, near the end of the interview, I repeatedly tell Lou to record a live comedy album. As it happens, he did take my advice and record an evening of standards 'n' stand-up: the comedy classic Take No Prisoners. *And, just as Lou had presciently predicted, the critics killed him for it.*

He gets no respect, I tell ya. No respect at all.

☆☆☆

PART ONE: THE DELICATE DELINQUENT

☆☆☆

LOU REED: Go ahead, interview me.

JEFFREY MORGAN: Y'know, I'm trying to wait until we get to a table.

REED: What does *this* look like?

MORGAN: This is a bar.

REED: It's better than a table. A table is a straight bar. [*looking around*] There's a table. I bet if we sit down, nobody'll say anything if it's really done discreetly…

WAITRESS: Would you like to order lunch now?

REED: We decided not to eat.

WAITRESS: Okay, so you're just going to stay here and have drinks?

REED: Right.

MORGAN: I want to do something—

REED: They've never done before.

MORGAN: No, something more definitive.

REED: [*looking over*] Can we order off of you, or are you here for looks?

WAITER: What would you like, sir?

REED: Can I have a Lowenbrau and a double scotch straight up, Johnny Walker Black?

MORGAN: Have you always been interested in sports?

REED: Yeah. Basketball and track, 'cause I wasn't big enough to play football. I was good to catch passes but…I hurt myself. This is true, believe it or not, but I was a pole vaulter, okay, and I landed wrong. The whole thing is in how you kick off, y'know, in the shoulders—and I had big shoulders. The kick, and then how you land 'cause if you land *wrong*, you can really…so I landed wrong.

We were in what they call a tri-semester—or a tri-county or something or other—and the really good pole vaulter had broken his leg. It looks easy if you do it right, and if you *don't* do it right they don't get to see you because you've broken something by that point and only maniacs would go out for that. But they asked me during the quarter finals so I was put in. And this is at eight foot six, and you can see how pathetic it is. At eight foot six which is, like, *nothing*. Nine and a half, ten feet is okay to fuck up, but at *eight foot six* to fuck up is just…

So I did 220 and I did pole vaulting. 220; that's easy, there's nothing to that, it's just running. I could do the hundred pretty good; the 220 wasn't bad. But pole vaulting I really wanted 'cause you gotta work on that. Just getting your kick right. And it's so embarrassing when you're starting out 'cause you look like a fool and the pole lands on top of you and it's knocking the bar on top of you and you're lying there in sawdust with everybody saying, "Schmuck! Look at the schmuck!" And the coach is yelling, "You're a fucking asshole; you're supposed to kick with the *right* foot and pull, not pull first and then kick with your left foot," 'cause then you'll get the bar right in your fucking balls.

So eight foot six is where they're *starting*. The other guy's passing, he's going to go in at ten feet, but for me— what's the highest *I've* ever done? And I'm a replacement anyway, so I went in, right? First two: pass, not happening. So, the third one, did it stupid. I tried harder which is *not* what you're supposed to do. You don't try harder in the sense of giving it a little extra pull. *Dumb*. That's the last . . . absolute first thing they teach you not to do. Don't do that. Don't try to do things out of, you know, thing. Because if you decide, "Now I'll give it a little extra…" And so that's what I did. And so I landed wrong and I just fucked my back up. From that point on I've got a fucked up back. Which goes right, it doesn't *stay* fucked up. So that's what happened.

The thing is, I *liked* that kind of shit. I was *into* it. One on one basketball. *Dirty*. I got thrown off the squad for getting into an argument with the basketball coach. I threw a basketball at him, actually. I didn't know he was watching and he saw it. I didn't throw it really at him, I threw it at the basket but I had it aimed so it would *rebound*, and he caught it. [*laughs*] He was dumb, but he was just smart enough to realize that I wasn't aiming for the hoop…and that's possibly because the hoop was *here*, and it was somehow hard to miss. And I was removed.

The thing was, I had a deadly fade away jump; one hand jump. Oh, *beautiful*. I'm one of those people who wanted a clean shot. I didn't want it to go off the board and go in. To show how downhill my neighborhood went, they didn't have cloth on the basketball rim, it was chains. You don't leave cloth up there because if the dogs don't get

it, the kids will.

There was a Suicide Strip where they had drag racing because there was a dead end. That was high school. I go back to when they had air raid drills. For fire drills you had to get in line, but for an air raid drill you had to get right under the desk, where I always found a used sandwich. Or somebody's Tampax, used. "Hey, I didn't know you used those yet."

There was always some guy who'd been left behind for twelve years named, you know, 'Ugh,' and Ugh had been in the tenth grade forever; since anyone could remember. He was the one you sent out for beer. He was a fixture, like a desk, and you sat in alphabetical rows. He once lifted me up by the head, for no reason in particular except I existed, and I was breathing, and I was within arm's reach. He just lifted me up and I remember thinking, "He's proved his point to me. I *really* understand. I understand the system now." And things haven't changed appreciably: there's always an Ugh behind you. *That'll* work its way into your article nicely: "There's Always An Ugh Behind You." But it's true. His name was Harold something—which, parenthetically, is the name of my sister's husband.

MORGAN: How do you spell 'Ugh'?

REED: U-G-H. Like the comic books.

MORGAN: The classic Ugh.

REED: Yeah, the classic Ugh. Ugh was something like Jughead, but not dumb.

MORGAN: A cross between Moose and Reggie?

REED: Yeah,

right. Jughead, if he'd been evil, would've looked like Carmen Sapilio, who was sitting in front of me for three grades in a row. I kept hoping he'd flunk. You know: R, S, Sapilio. There you go. Could *not* get rid of him no matter what I did. Three years. Through orthodontia; the most awful moments of your life when you want to be alone. And you're saying, "Aw, please, have a heart…" And there's Ugh on one side and Sapilio on the other. Terrible.

We had these classic guys. The classroom monitor or the hall monitor, who was going to run for president some day when he was really smart. And he'd gotten 99 in algebra so everybody really hated his guts. "*Fucking fairy. He's a fucking fairy, man. Fucking asshole cocksucker, he's a fucking fairy*."

And I got Brock Peters in front of me. Walked into the john once, and he says, "You know what a blow job is?"

WAITER: Anything to drink or some appetizers?

REED: [*laughs*] Talk about a cue. If he'd come in with a tennis racket and said—

MORGAN: "Tennis anyone?"

REED: [*laughs*] Yeah. What a place for a line like that. [*to waiter*] Can I have a little spareribs?

MORGAN: Can I have a toasted chicken sandwich?

REED: Can I have a clothes dryer 'cause I came. I'm wet.

No, really: *Ughs*. What an album title. *Songs About Ughs I Have Known*. Do I love it? Do I love it? *Ughs I Have Known*, Lou Reed. My next album, right? A song for every Ugh.

☆☆☆

PART TWO: AT WAR WITH THE ARMY

☆☆☆

MORGAN: What did you do in your off time when you weren't in high school?

REED: Played basketball.

MORGAN: Was that it?

REED: Yeah. And played in rock 'n' roll bands.

MORGAN: When did you start with the rock 'n' roll?

REED: Oh, I was doing that all along. It was the only way I could get accepted. It was the only way I could make money and not have the bad guys beat me to death. Really. It's really true.

Anyway, I was standing in the john and this guy came in and said, "What's a blow job?" "Gee, I don't know." And he says: [*puffs lightly three times*] And what's sick is *I believed him*. I went up to my best friend Dickie Green and I said, "What is [*puffs lightly three times*]? I bet *you* don't know." And he said, "A blow job, schmuck." I was *ruined* 'cause I wasn't getting off on it.

MORGAN: So you went home and you played guitar.

REED: That's what got me into my guitar. I got a... Oh, what's the hippie guitar to have that everybody started out with first? And I actually *had* one.

MORGAN: Kent?

REED: I *had* a Kent. *Before* I had the Kent. Worse yet.

MORGAN: A Martin?

REED: No, NO, *NO*, no, no. The D28? Never. *NEVER!* Silk on steel with finger picks? Uh-uh, no. I *had* a Kent, but previous to the Kent. It starts with an H and it's not a Hohner. A Harmony. No, it wasn't a Harmony. Oh, I paid five bucks for it if you can believe it. A *Stella*. It *doesn't* start with an H. I had a Stella, an old Stella with Black Diamond strings on it. That shows I really know what I'm talking about. And I had a Gretch. It was a grey Gretch. It wasn't even the right one; the White Falcon, which is the only Gretch to get. I was using the wrong strings. They didn't have good strings on. I tried to transmogrify—how's *that* for one— Black Diamond strings to an electric. I even went to the banjo at one point and learned how to flail.

MORGAN: John McLaughlin's doing that on his new album...

REED: Ohhhh, *sp*—

MORGAN: ...with a guitar synthesizer.

REED: Up his ass. *Please*.

MORGAN: Don't listen to it.

REED: I haven't. Ever. He can have his bun and burger at home, but he's not... Never records, ne—

"Go get some boys from Brian." That's Epstein in T.O. The only thing nice about Brian Epstein is that he has Spanish servants who *can't speak English*, that's the joke, get it? No? Okay, we'll just keep running them down...

MORGAN: How could such a nice guy like you get kicked out of ROTC for threatening to shoot an officer?

REED: [*laughs*] Without bullets in the rifle.

MORGAN: It was a rifle?

REED: Yeah. I was in ROTC for a month. I was a platoon leader. This is true. The reason this happened is because they said, "*This row*," and I couldn't get out of the row fast enough; they got me. I was a platoon leader so I had to get out of the Army. I would've been an officer.

MORGAN: How old were you when this happened?

REED: When I went to college. Uh, I must've been...what was I? I was seventeen.

MORGAN: You were that fed up with it.

REED: *Yeah*. They wanted me to block my hat. [*laughs*] I'm serious. You have to have your hat all polished and blocked. Like if people've stamped on it and the inside's caved in, in the middle, and it's all bent…

MORGAN: Oh, you've got to take a hammer and—

REED: *Right*. You're supposed to put paper inside and really mould it…

MORGAN: Kinda like packing china.

REED: Right. Exactly. So I waited until my turn came up to be platoon leader and I walked into the office with a rifle.

MORGAN: An unloaded rifle.

REED: Yeah. They didn't give us bullets yet. That doesn't come 'till later, *way* later.

MORGAN: And what did you say to this guy?

REED: I said, "I'm going to *shoot* you if you don't throw me out of ROTC." He was so…*astonished*. I caught him off guard.

MORGAN: Was he scared or was it just disbelief that—

REED: Both. He was initially scared 'cause you don't react logically when somebody comes waltzing in with a rife, threatening to shoot you. I ended up being rejected by the Army when I finally *did* get drafted.

MORGAN: Was it because of the bad back?

REED: No, it was a combination of anti-social behavior and being mentally unfit. The definition of a manic depressive is: "As high as you go is as low as you go, therefore you've experienced energy and beauty." Being a manic depressive is like having brown hair, you just have it. Just like being skinny or fat, it just is. Like having brown eyes. If you're a manic depressive, that's it, you just are. It's no big deal. And one of the peripheral effects is that as high as you go is as low as you go. Two ways of taking that.

MORGAN: And when you hit the bottom, you know that you can look up.

REED: You know what up *is*. And you can experience energy and beauty. Delmore Schwartz said that. He was a great man.

MORGAN: What's the lowest you can go?

REED: The highest. As high as you went, that's as low as you can go. He also said, "Power corrupts absolutely. Absolute power corrupts absolutely. All great men are insane."

MORGAN: Would you take any of it back?

REED: What?

MORGAN: Your life. Would you change it?

REED: No, are you *kidding?*

MORGAN: Would you do it again?

REED: No one's *asked* me. [*chuckles*] Y'know, like He hasn't come down with a sheet of paper saying, "You wanna go to the seventh floor again?" *Pass.* It hasn't happened. It's like there's been a demolition derby. "I'm locked in a closet without the key and the house does not belong to me." Far out. [*laughs and takes a drink*]

MORGAN: Are you scared of death?

REED: [*gagging on his drink*] *Are you serious?* [*laughter*] Having only experienced it twice myself, I can say offhand *it's not that bad*. I'm starting to get *into* it, as a matter of fact… [*laughter*]

MORGAN: When you close your eyes for the last time, do you expect to go somewhere?

REED: As was said to me, "When I go into a place, hopefully far better than

this, if you sell out, I'll haunt you." Delmore said that to me. He was very drunk and he thought he was Leopold Bloom and I was Stephen Dedalus. And those were his last words that I ever got out of him: "You sell out, I'll haunt you." If it's possible. And if anybody could do it, *he* could.

MORGAN: How can you get up in the morning after all you've seen, all you've been through? What keeps you alive? Really? You must—

REED: The constant throbbing of effervescent hope that keeps bubbling inside me like coagulating wheat germ.

MORGAN: You're trying to tell me that?

REED: What keeps me going?

MORGAN: Is it the glory of love that stops you from jumping out a window?

REED: Absolutely. Absolutely. That, or I would become a vicious creature of the sea.

MORGAN: A lesser man would be dead by now.

REED: A lesser man wouldn't have gotten that *far*. Or he would have gone behind the scenes very, very quickly… which I may do.

Jimmy Smith: He was the all-time thief in New York for a while until he tried to steal somebody's guitar. I think it was the guy from the Chad Mitchell Trio, and they threw him out of a fourth story window. Him and his dog. "Try walking out *there*, you A-head!"

It's like when Andrea Feldman committed suicide, she jumped out the window and said she was trying for the big time. And she… Like, the only thing anybody in New York ever had to mention about her was that she landed *so hard* in the sidewalk that she left footprints. I was gonna say *hoofprints*, I dunno why. But it must've been 'cause it was a tragedy for a cow or a horse. Andrea Feldman. That's not romantic. She changed it to Andrea Warhol.

> ## Critics treat me like dirt!
> ### - Lou Reed

MORGAN: Wasn't it "Whips"?

REED: [*surprised*] Yeah, as a matter of fact. Andrea "Whips" Feldman.

MORGAN: Do you feel safe? Do you feel secure?

REED: Oh, I am.

MORGAN: As secure as you can get?

REED: For a person like me? Yeah. Sure. Having experienced the heights of insecurity, what can they do to me at *this* point?

MORGAN: Well, they seem to be having a campaign to delete all your albums.

REED: *I* don't care. How's that hurt me? It makes it better.

MORGAN: *You* don't care? *You're* the one who's going around saying you dyed your hair blonde so you could get all the Velvets' stuff back in print.

REED: Yeah, but I *did* it. That's all over.

MORGAN: So now if they delete them again, you've proved your point.

REED: Yeah, proint proved.

MORGAN: "Proint proved"?

REED: Prawns. "Only a prawn in their game." Now if he'd done that, *that* would have been hip. [*laughs*] "With only pot on our side, you're only a prawn in their game."

MORGAN: That's the way it goes, though.

REED: Bebe Rebozo?

MORGAN: No, Joey Gallo, the guy that Dylan sings about—

REED: Oh, is that the put-on song of the… I love it, he *is* joking, he's got—

MORGAN: I don't know—

REED: No, he's—

MORGAN: If he's serious—

REED: No, he can't be. No, he can't be. It's gotta be *his* idea of a goof. He *can't* be serious.

MORGAN: I don't think the "Hurricane" thing was serious, either.

REED: I don't think so, either. Let Dylan have some racist slurs. *Imagine* him, running around, trying to find some nigger in jail, saying, "*I'm doing a benefit*, somebody find… Where are the Rosenbergs when I need them? Somebody *do* something." [*in Dylan's voice*] "*Hey!*"

MORGAN: Somebody once asked you if you were influenced by Dylan and you said, "Are you kidding?"

REED: Well, I mean, *be serious*. I mean, *really*. Talk about aspersions on a character. I was asked to go on the Rolling Thunder Review, but I had the clap. No? Moving on…

MORGAN: Did you ever catch—

REED: Many times.

MORGAN: …one of his Reviews?

REED: No, I was asked to join, though. By proxy. Ever make love by proxy?

MORGAN: The first time I heard *Berlin* was on a Saturday night at two in the morning—

REED: And you felt sad and guilty and you want to put it off on me? [*sings*] "How do you think it…" An anthem to the rising sun, as seen from the opposing side of the moon. One of the great, one of the great… I mean, they released it as a single. Fools.

☆☆☆

PART THREE: THE FAMILY JEWELS

☆☆☆

MORGAN: Critics treat you like—

REED: *LIKE DIRT!!!* They fucking treat me like… [*theatrically muttering to himself*] *Y'know…if you can't keep it together…*

MORGAN: The audience wasn't treating you so good either the last time you were here. When you were in last time, and you did—

REED: I was *out* last time, but…

MORGAN: When you were out and on last time, doing—

REED: My thing.

MORGAN: "Kicks" and "Coney Island" and "I Want To Be Black" and all that—

REED: Doing what?

MORGAN: "I Want To Be Black."

REED: What'd I do? Is that what I was

doing?

MORGAN: As far as I can remember it.

REED: What is *that* supposed to mean?

MORGAN: It means it was one of the best solo shows I ever saw, whether you remember it or not.

REED: Y'see, the thing is, I *don't* remember it. But I always like playing Toronto.

MORGAN: Yeah, and it was a great show for—

REED: [*laughing*] I… I'm serious, I'm not… [*laughs*] *Why do people not believe me?* I *try* to tell the truth. I'm saying at that time we were traveling around so much I can't differentiate shows in my head. Y'know, past a certain point, it turns into a blur.

MORGAN: I'm just saying it was a great show, but the audience was screaming out "Vicious." They wanted the rock 'n' roll animal and you were telling them to kiss off 'cause you were trying to do the new stuff.

REED: Oh, you should hear a tape of the Felt Forum. One *long* fight and finally it erupts midway through the show. Confrontation. Lay down the guitars. Start playing cards with the guys. I was doing things like "I Want To Be Black." I finally told the audience that, "Hey, this is my trip." And they start yelling and screaming. It's so fucking funny.

People are saying, "You're really fucking lucky you didn't get a brick in the head." The thing is, I've *never* gotten hit with anything…except in Italy, and that's because of a post office election, of all fucking things. I don't get any credit for it. They had a riot in Italy. Two riots. And we were involved in it only in the sense that we happened to unfortunately *be* there.

And in the States it was reported that it was because of the music and the morality I represented, yak yak yak yak yak. Y'know: bourgeois and degeneracy. And the thing was, they had a post office clerk election and the Communists wanted attention so they happened to have a rock concert. So they disrupted it. And it turned into a *really* scary thing. Y'know, bricks really *were* flying. Gas masks, tear grenades, the whole thing. Seven people in the hospital, the troops…

MORGAN: That's ridiculous.

REED: Oh yeah, the fucking wops…

MORGAN: There's a lot of people running around without any brains and you always seem to come up against those people specifically; the ones who

don't have any idea of what they're doing.

REED: I happen to attract them like, uh, *flies*. It's incredible. Not that I mind it, but I *do*. It's like Yeats: "The best lack all conviction while the worst are filled with a passionate intensity." The ones with the least to say are the noisiest. So what happens in New York is that the ones with the least to say are *screaming* and yelling and everything and the other people can't hear anything, and so I'm playing softer just to make sure so that it's gotta come to a confrontation. 'Cause I said, "This is my trip."

MORGAN: It was edging to that the last time you were here.

REED: Oh, yeah, well in New York it happened.

MORGAN: Well, it was a great show, anyway. It was infinitely better than when you were running around with the blonde hair.

REED: Oh, that was my way of *also*

> ## "
> *Eddie Fisher is being flown in to produce my new album.*
>
> **- Lou Reed**
> "

telling them to jerk off, but they *liked* it.

MORGAN: Yeah, well, I thought that you looked like an ass. That's why I was so happy to see you up there doing your songs the way *you* wanted to do them. But the audience wanted to see the jerk in the blonde hair dancing around and aborting all of his original material.

REED: That's what they wanted though, so that's what they got. Well, you saw what happened when they got what they *didn't* want; what *you* wanted…

MORGAN: You comin' in again on the twelfth of April to do your annual show?

REED: No.

MORGAN: Whaddya mean, *no?* I hear you're coming in on the twelfth. You gonna lie to me?

REED: *You heard wrong*. I'm not coming in on the twelfth.

MORGAN: You're not coming in?

REED: No.

MORGAN: You're not doing a show?

REED: No. I cancelled it. No, they had it booked for the twelfth, apparently. But it was a tentative booking.

MORGAN: Why don't you come in?

REED: 'Cause I don't *want* to.

MORGAN: That's a good enough answer.

REED: That's a *real* answer.

MORGAN: Is there actually a black photo on—

REED: *Yeah*.

MORGAN: 'Cause I can see it. If you put it under the light, there's a blue gradation…

REED: It depends if you have the original album because the original album had a black on black photo. You know, it was Joe Dellasandro's sh… No, it wasn't Joe Dellasandro, it was a motorcyclist's shoulder with a death's head tattoo. With skull and crossbones. Switchblade between his teeth. And it was a black on black photo, but the copies that are out *now* are just a black cover.

But the original black on black photo, there'd be people who didn't even know it was there until they took the cellophane off, like, a year later and they'd be high on acid. And they'd suddenly say: "*AHHHHHHHHH!!!* What *is* that?"

MORGAN: Are you happy with this new one? I've been reading all the interviews and you've been saying—

REED: Oh, *Coney Island Baby*?

MORGAN: Yeah.

REED: Absolutely.

MORGAN: 'Cause you're a notorious liar. Just from what I've read—and it may not be you, it may be the journalists—but I've read so much and there's always five different versions on each topic and—

REED: Oh, let's just talk about us then. *Coney Island Baby* I really love from top to bottom, period.

MORGAN: If I can detract for a minute about *Metal Machine*—

REED: Feel the same way. It's the other side of the coin. Outside of those two and *Berlin*—

MORGAN: Yeah, but the other side of the coin is: There's a statement just out this month saying the only reason you did them was to get out of your contract. Now what the hell's a guy like me supposed to believe when the only contact he's got with you is through the records and the magazines?

REED: Just 'cause it might get me out of the contract doesn't mean I don't love it. I mean, it's not antithetical.

MORGAN: It was worded as saying, "That's the only reason why I did it."

REED: *Oh, no*. That's not true. I mean, *that's just not true*. I love Metal Machine. I *also* love Coney Island

Baby. So that's the problem when I say, "Oh, I *really* love this record," 'cause I have to preface it by saying, "But I *also* love *Metal Machine*." So there's a problem. But I love *Coney Island Baby* as much.

MORGAN: If you had the power to delete any of your albums, which ones would go into the furnace?

REED: *Lou Reed, Transformer, Rock n Roll Animal, Lou Reed Live, Sally Can't Dance*… [*pauses*] Did I *miss* any? Mainly *Sally Can't Dance*, especially. Well, I would save parts of *Transformer*. And the first *Lou Reed* album, that was legitimate. But the musicians, no. It's wretchedly produced. If I could save the songs on there but throw away the record…

MORGAN: Sort of re-record them?

REED: Yeah. Just have the album vanish and do all the songs again without anybody knowing. I mean, some of the best songs I ever *wrote* are on that fucking album, y'know. Nobody knows it. "Wild Child." I mean, that was *oh!* That's such a fantastic song, I can't believe it. And "Ride Into The Sun." I *love* that.

MORGAN: I love "Ocean."

REED: Yeah, but I didn't, didn't, didn't

do it right. Didn't, didn't get it. On *Lou Re*… On Mercury *Velvet Underground Live*, got "Ocean" much better.

MORGAN: You can't get that in Canada, you know. You gotta buy that on Import.

REED: Oh, you're *kidding*. That's probably one of the… That has the only real "Sweet Jane" on it. That's the best album—

MORGAN: Was that really done the night, the day you wrote it?

REED: *Yeah*, I mean—

MORGAN: 'Cause I love the bit with the "Days Of Wine And Roses." That is *so* poignant.

REED: On *Loaded*, on fucking *Loaded* they…y'know, 'cause I had to fucking split and they *edited out the whole fucking ending* and they—

MORGAN: You mean you *recorded* it like that?

REED: Yeah. Yeah. That whole part is on there and they cut it off. And the thing is, on *Max's Kansas City* you can hear that part's on there. The thing is, the tempo and the lyrics on *1969*…

"New Age" for instance; the way they edited it out on *Loaded* again, and you hear, like, it had a long ending? *Aw, man*… "New Age" was another of my masterpieces. Literally. The thing is, I consciously butchered "Heroin" and "Sweet Jane" on purpose and just said, "That's what the little clowns want."

MORGAN: You mean for the *Rock n Roll Animal* stuff?

REED: Yeah. And people say, "How come you don't like it?"

MORGAN: It's a great guitar album.

REED: That's what it *is*.

MORGAN: It's a great rock album.

REED: For what it is, for that kind of thing, if you go for that, it's probably up there with the best. Like, that's why I like the *Lou Reed Live* album, because of the Hunter-Wagner duel on "Oh, Jim." I think that's superb. But "Heroin," y'know, with that *intro*… But it's great for heavy metal nonsense. It's like being in a time warp.

MORGAN: It's the Velvets. It's the Mercury album, and you can't get it up here.

REED: That's *obscene* that you can't get it up here.

MORGAN: As a matter of fact, you can't get the Max's one, either.

REED: That's a *classic*.

MORGAN: I had to shell out eight bucks for that one, too.

REED: It's *worth* it, because it's the

only way you can *ever* know what Max's was like for real on a Sunday night with the house band which was, *who else?* Who else could've *possibly* survived there? Jim Carroll trying to get Tuinals… I mean, it's *priceless*.

MORGAN: I loved the way they had to stamp "Mono" on all the original copies.

REED: They *had* to put a thing on it. We talked them into it, too. We said, "Hey, it'll be your first legal bootleg. Isn't that hip? Isn't that hip?" *Really, really*. Love it.

Some kid came up to me in Cleveland showing me these old records, I don't know how he fucking got them, on Pickwick International when I was a songwriter there and we were doing things like "Johnny Can't Surf No More" and "I've Got A Tiger In My Tank."

> "
>
> *I'm the Don Rickles of rock.*
>
> - Lou Reed
>
> "

MORGAN: You're kidding me.

REED: No, they're *fantastic* songs. By the way, you should get *Metal Machine*. Like the only *real* way to hear it, the whole point of the whole thing—

MORGAN: I've *got Metal Machine*.

REED: No, but in *discreet matrix* they call it.

MORGAN: I can't find a copy!

REED: I've got *one*.

MORGAN: I've searched all over—

REED: They're very rare, to say the least. Y'know, in New York, the thing is banned. Not banned, I mean—

MORGAN: Gone to the furnaces.

REED: Well, it's not available, but it's a collector's item already. People are paying, like, fifteen bucks to get the fucking thing 'cause it's like Warhol's soup can. It was. It's not the real quad. It's the quad that you can play on a stereo and they call it discreet matrix. You get the quad sound and it's *so* ferocious. I mean that's the *real* one that me and Ludwig…he helped me master it. I had to fight to get the

motherfucker out so bad.

Y'know, they say, "If they put you in a time capsule, Reed, what would you take with you?" *They go*. [laughs] *Metal Machine*. I would take that and I'd take *Coney Island Baby*. I really would. People think I'm jiving them, but I'm not. I'm really not.

MORGAN: That album performs a service, at certain times. When you *need* it, it's *there*.

REED: *Metal Machine*? When I need to get it out of my system so I don't *kill* somebody…it gets things out of my system. It's cathartic. I mean, it just sets my mind going in so many different directions. It's like being stoned. It *is*. I don't make no bones about it. "It sounds like Reed's circulatory system." *Oh!* All right, cheap, cheap one. I really *like* that thing. Also, I don't have it *in* me to make another one; it took way too long to make *that* one. But the idea was good enough. That's what I meant, like, it's like Andy's soup can.

Promo men across the *country* hate me. Can you imagine a guy running up to an AM station or an FM progressive?

"Here's Lou Reed's latest."

"Uh, what's the single?" [*clears his throat*]

Like, the *Billboard* review was great: "Recommended cuts: there *aren't* any. Sounds like: car static." You got it, you're closing in on it, c'mon, keep comin', keep comin'. Come on over here where the water's a little colder. I'd give anything to see the guy saying:

"Oh! Jeeze, the cover looks like…*he's gotta be kidding. What* does that say inside?"

Just for the liner notes…just for the—

"My week beats your year? *Whoa!* He's advocating *what*? In *slang terms*? Needles like *toothbrushes*? C'mon! Get serious. How did this get by RCA?"

Y'know *how*? 'Cause I said to them, "But the liner notes are *closed*, the little kiddies won't…the little buggers won't be able to *see* the motherfucking thing. It'll just…oh!…but as long as it's closed…just keep 'em sealed. And just say they've gotta hear two minutes of it before they buy it." That's what *I* had said.

MORGAN: I *went* to the record stores. I *tried* that. They wouldn't even *play* it

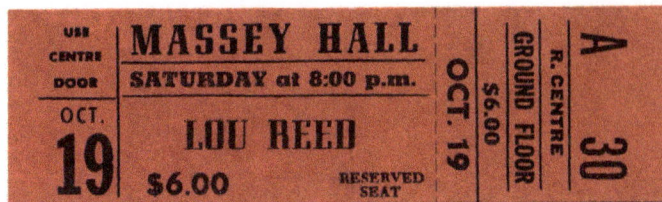

for me.

REED: [*dies of laughter*]

MORGAN: What's your personal opinion now of "Billy" on *Sally*?

REED: It was like, four songs for you and one for me. Like, "Ennui" was for me; "Billy" was for me…but by the time they got done with it again, you got lost someplace.

MORGAN: I see the thread between "Billy," "Coney Island Baby," the autobiographical material where you can, if you want to, read between the lines and see things.

REED: Yeah, if you want to. But keep it to yourself. Like, that's not asking much. Like, if *I* put it between the lines, y'know…and that's where it *is*: between the lines. *Way* between the lines. It's like, you know, a little "Hello" on those schlock records. That's my only way of saying: "Hi…hold on for a while…like, hopefully…have… prudence…"

☆☆☆

PART FOUR: PARDNERS

☆☆☆

MORGAN: Bowie was in town last month. He did a *horrendous* job of "I'm Waiting For The Man"…

REED: But he *did* it. Don't people *understand*? Don't people understand that he's doing it for himself? The kids out there don't know from that. He knows enough to know about it, David. He's just doing it *anyway*. Give fucking…give the guy a *break*.

It's just that, y'know, there's no…he can't win in this situation. The diehard Lou Reed fans are gonna sit there and put him down and the other people are going to say, "What the fuck is he doing?" They wanna hear "Stay" or they wanna hear "Golden Years," they don't want to hear *that* shit. They don't even know what he's talking about. So, man, the guy's got nothing to lose. I mean, he's got nothing he can fucking gain. He really doesn't. He's doing it… it's *his* way of saying, "Hello."

STAGE PASS
Access All Areas

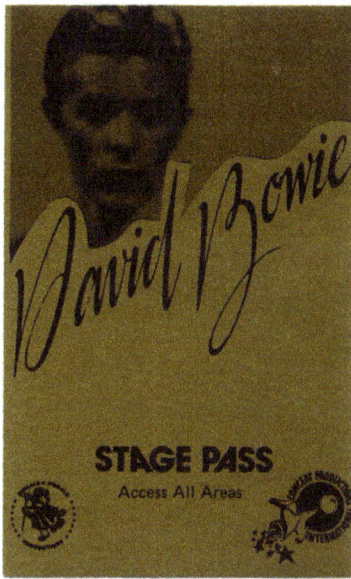

Y'know, you ought to grant him the fucking privilege, man. It drives me *crazy*, people going out after David when he's trying to… Like, man, it pisses me off, you have *no* idea. Like, why else would he do the song? Because people will think it's hip? *They* don't know. The most he might be able to do is like, by jiving his way through it—and he's *still* doing it. Man. *Hey*, man, that's David, y'know.

Like, some kid'll come outta there and say:

"What was that thing he did over there?"

"Oh, that's Lou Reed."

"Well, if David did it, maybe I should buy a Lou Reed album."

Okay? *Hey*, bottom line, man: *that's* what David's doing, you understand? Like, *you* already got it. But everybody *else*… You don't understand where he's coming from, man. He gets the shaft from the people who should *know* better, who should say, "Son of a bitch, like, he's making his move and he's trying to get some of them thrown on Lou."

MORGAN: *He's* doing the same thing *you're* doing. There're a lot of parallels between the moves that he's making—

REED: *Besides that*. But I'm saying if he did a thing like, "This is a song that Lou Reed wrote and I want you all to go get his record" and everything and, "This is a tribute" and everything, that would be the worst thing he could do in the *world*. The *worst*. That would be, like, the kiss of death. And *he* knows it, he *knows* it.

Doing it right is to put it over so the bulk of those kids don't wanna *kill* him onstage for wasting their time with a song they don't even know—that he didn't even *write*—that's not even on a *record* he's done. Don't you fucking *understand*? Don't you understand that? What's he up there, doing that? Fucking David. He's up there and he's doing this thing. *They've* never heard it, it's not on any album, they don't know *what* the fuck he's doing. But if he came out and *said* what he's doin', that would be the worst thing in the world for him and for me in particular.

Why was he doing it? He must *really* like the song, he's done it in every fucking show he's *done*. He must *really* like it a hell of a lot. He must like the guy who did it a hell of a lot. One or the other, or both. He wasn't going for you. He figured you're smart enough and if you're not, that it can't hurt him to help me and to help him, like, keep his own sanity.

Man, don't knock Bowie. Don't knock his motives. How could you put a negative motive to it? What has he got to gain at this stanza? Seriously, man, it's not fair. I mean, it's *that* kind of thinking that has people on *me*, just from the other side. "He didn't do it exactly the way you did." Or: "He didn't do it right where he really believed it, he was jive-assing through—"

He's jive-assing through *all* his songs, for that matter.

It's not fair, man. It's not fair to fucking David. Anybody who could do "New York Telephone Conversation" with me which is, like, *the* one on *Transformer*, and made more enemies for a one minute song… That created more hassle for both me and him than you can *ever* imagine 'cause the people it was aimed at were listening: New York yentas. You'll never know.

He did "Walk On The Wild Side" with me. *Our* hit. Aw, David… He's gone through hell and he still is. Whatever he's going through—which he knows better than anybody else and I wouldn't even presume to talk about it—but you can't, you can't *fault* him.

"It's not the sad eff…it's not the side effects of the cocaine, I'm thinking that it must be love." *Oh*. "It's too late to be

late again. It's too late to be grateful. It's too late to be hateful." Oh, man, have a heart, what's *wrong* with you? It's not fair. "*It's too late*." I mean, dig where *he's* coming from: "It's too late to be late again." [*whistles*] Y'know, really.

"Hey, Dave—"

"I don't wanna take drugs, they slow me down."

"Right. Meet you at the point. Meet you at the mountain top, see you around. Did you see the volcano?"

"No, we're shining. Blue moon."

"Later."

Aw, don't do that. Like, "If You Rock And Roll With Me," you ever listen to *that* song? *Saddest* song in the *world*. I mean as—

MORGAN: I always thought that "Quicksand" was one of the saddest songs in the world.

REED: Martha and the Vandellas?

MORGAN: No, his. On *Hunky Dory*? "Sinking in the quicksand of my thoughts"?

REED: "Bewlay Brothers." "I was stone and he was wax so he could scream and still relax, unbelievable. And we frightened the small children away." [*whistles*] Hey. "He's chameleon, comedian, Corinthian and caricature."

I mean, c'mon, that's no hobo talking over here. That's no idiot. "That he could scream and still relax, unbelievable." And *nobody* ever *noticed* that. And the song before it is called "Queen Bitch," and guess who it's dedicated to? "Oh, I could do better than that in my flippity, flippity, flippity, floppity hat." Guess who? *Bitch*.

MORGAN: Who?

REED: David. Well, if he could say it about *me*…

Now I'll play David on *The Dick Cavett Show*.

[*slouches in his chair towards the floor, shaking violently and thrashing his hands like a paraplegic having an epileptic seizure*]

[*in Bowie's voice*] "Yes, Dick. Ahhhhhh*hahhhhhh* [*bangs on table*] No, I don't do anything. [*yanks at himself*] Sit *up*! An-*gie*! [*pounds his leg with his fist*] Make the kid stop! Zowie! Bite my toes off!"

[*sits up and laughs*]

David's such fun.

Angie's American, everybody should always remember that. I feel sorry for David. With an American bitch like that, how can you *help* but be a success? Push, push, push.

☆☆☆

PART FIVE: HARDLY WORKING

☆☆☆

REED: Where are the fun bars to go to around here?

MORGAN: What do you mean by *fun*? One man's fun is another man's torture chamber.

REED: It's like sitting on a hot totem pole. You know, some of the ancient tortures were out of sight. They'd put you on a long bamboo pole about *that wide* [*gestures*] with a point, right up your ass, greased. And you're tied like that. And they'd sit you on top and you'd slide down and it'd *pop* right up the top of your head. Then there's another one.

MORGAN: [*delayed groan*]

REED: There's another one. They'd make you eat rice that was uncooked and you'd have to swallow a lot of hot water. And the rice would, like, from boiling water you'd have that [*makes crackling sounds*]. And your *stomach* would burst, 'cause it's like popcorn, except it was rice. They call it the rice torture. Otherwise know as Trader Vic's thing…

"Can I have a rice torture?"

[*in a Chinese voice*] "We don't have a white boy yet."

MORGAN: What *I* want to know is:

When are you going to put out a live comedy album?

REED: I've been doing comedy albums for the *longest* time. I've been saying, "Folks, I'm not serious." I'm one of those people who usually gets involved in fights in a bar, even when it's not crowded. I'll find somebody…

MORGAN: The bartender?

REED: No, they're used to me now.

MORGAN: What is it? The frustrations?

REED: No, I was always like that. I'm an incipient wise guy.

MORGAN: You're a latent comedian.

REED: It's not latent, it's blatant. Overt, not invert. Disparaging, not despairing. Stop before I kill again…

MORGAN: That's a great title for an album.

REED: I gave the guy from the *Toronto Star* a good title. I don't know if he writes his own work. "Lou, what is the street corner influence that's manifested in this album? I mean, did you call it *Coney Island Baby* for a reason?" No, I called it that for *no* reason.

[*looking up at the ceiling*] What *is* that by the way? I was just curious. Is it moving down or is that my drink? There are *skulls* up there. Warhol just did the greatest paintings of some skulls. I mean, they're just incredible.

MORGAN: That's the next step to go. Just take the flesh off and get to what's really there.

REED: No, they're *really nice*.

MORGAN: You oughtta do a live comedy album.

REED: Who, me?

MORGAN: But you gotta do it in the *right place*, yeah. The critics would slice you to pieces, but—

REED: Oh, I'd get *killed*. But I *made* an album once, just for myself. Like, it was songs, but mainly rapping, y'know. And making up songs like, uh, [*singing*] "Yoga's an amphetamine." *And nobody laughed*.

"Is he serious?"

"No, he's not serious, no."

[*singing*] "What's an Andy Warhol doll? Wind it up and it does nothing. *Nothing?* Nothing. *Nothing?* Nothing."

MORGAN: Isn't that supposed to be… I read that was a quote from the adaptation of *Andy From A To B And Back Again*.

REED: That was an old joke.

MORGAN: Yeah, but are you going to

adapt it into the book?

REED: Oh yeah, I've got the whole thing for the book *done*. And the thing is, like, that's what I'd *really* like to do. I mean, it's all done. It's two hours' worth. Oh, you should…the songs take it… That *really* should be my new album. Like, fuck 'em all.

MORGAN: But you keep on—

REED: I keep on *what*?

MORGAN: You keep on fluctuating. First you put out a crappy album, and then you follow it up with a good one. You go up and you go down and you go up and you go down.

REED: Well, you only know that you're up when you're down.

MORGAN: But how long are you going to keep people stringing after you?

REED: What do *I* give a fuck? I put out, y'know, what I *want* to . . .

MORGAN: Then why do you come to Toronto to do these interviews?

REED: Because I did the album. Going back to the *beginning* of our conversation, Fred… Like, uh, Fred is the kind of name… Somebody named Fred has to be *dumb*. But it's *not true*, it's just—

MORGAN: What about Frank?

REED: Franks? You gotta…they're not brilliant but, y'know…

MORGAN: What about Lou?

REED: Lous are crafty. A Lou can be anything, y'know. Like Francis or John. And a john can be a man's best friend.

MORGAN: [*silence*]

REED: [*whistles the sound of a bomb falling from a B-29*] Anyway… No? Okay, we'll leave that alone. Moving ever onward…

MORGAN: You'd be great on a Dean Martin roast, man. I could see you up there, right?

REED: [*laughs*] The Don Rickles of rock. I'm trying to push that as my new—

MORGAN: Is that your new image? Is that the new one?

REED: Yeah, well, not the Sammy Davis Jr. That's one nigger we *don't* need.

Anyway, *Coney Island Baby* I truly believe in one hundred percent, unlike all my other albums, with the exception of *Berlin*—which was a combination of attempts to make something worthwhile happen—and *Metal Machine* which I am responsible for from the beginning to the end in conception and packaging and the cover. Just like *Coney Island Baby* they

PART SIX:
THE KING OF COMEDY

☆☆☆

REED: I had an interview on an FM progressive station in New York with the morning DJ and I'm thinking: What am I *doing* here with an interview? I said, "Who is your listening audience out there?" He said, "Well, I'm on at six-thirty in the morning."

I said, "Well, my people are just *coming down* then. Or else they're *crying*. I never see the sun from that point of view, I'm coming from the other direction."

"They're usually showering, they don't even hear me, they just—"

I said, "They just hear the bass and drum, I know, let me guess."

Six-thirty in the morning and he said to me, "I dominate the conversation, that's the one rule." During the interview they said the pauses were too long between the questions and answers—or between word and word, in my case. Like, I would go, "Oh." [*long pause*] And we'd be good for, like, a half hour. And the interview is supposed to be just a five minute spot, broadcast once while they were in the shower jerking off or fucking a parr...or fucking terriers.

He said, "We've gotta edit his pauses down. He speaks awfully low, doesn't he?"

I said, "I'm not *tall* enough for you?"

"Let's cut another one, we'll edit it."

I said, "You can't edit anything I say out of context."

"We're not doing that. We're taking the pauses out."

"Well, that's out of context." If you have a joke, timing is of the essence.

MORGAN: Pacing.

REED: Pacing, right. And they were destroying the pacing.

MORGAN: They didn't see the humor in it though, right?

REED: *Not at all.* I mean, the guy is sitting there... "This is off the record. Are we on? No. Gee, you know, I live down on Tenth Avenue in the Chelsea section and there're all these creeps running around in leather clothing and they look at me oddly but I know that, y'know, they're not interested 'cause I wear a *fluffy sweater!* Aw-haw-haw-haw! And *sneakers* that are *red!*"

are the flip side of each other; two antithetical poles it would seem, but no, this is not true. Like, from one end of the spectrum to the other, if it was a Richter scale from one to ten, one might be *Metal Machine* and *Coney Island Baby* and, on the other end at ten, you would have either *Metal Machine* and *Coney Island Baby* and anything in between that I have total control of, as well as the next album that I *also* have total control of, so I can now do whatever I *want* to do, which is why I did *Sally Can't Dance* and the rest of the bullshit.

MORGAN: Thank you, Mr. Lou Reed of New York City.

REED: I'll be running for congress next May...

MORGAN: Why don't you go into the studio next time with a guitar—

REED: You know how many people wanna tape me doing this stuff? *Andy From A To B And Back Again.* I would love to do it.

MORGAN: You *oughtta* do it.

REED: I've *done* it, I've got the *tapes.* I've got tapes, I've got letters, I've got feathers, I've got baubles...

MORGAN: Put it out.

REED: "It's either in the grooves or it's not." I love industry talk. I remember, like, when I was a young kid: "Let's fly it up the pole and see if the flag waves."

I said, "Gee...is *that* how commerce works? Is *that* what it's all about? *Fly it up the pole?* What are they *talking* about? Ladies' lingerie? I saw a Jack Lemmon movie, is *that* what it's about?"

And then you have Ugh going, "*NO!*"

And I'm sitting there saying, "Are they those funny ones with the funny name? Xanxus, the Olympic ones?" I'm playing Lou Reed now. [*he picks up his sunglasses, which he doesn't notice are bent out of shape at the bridge*] I'm playing Lou Reed…gotta put on… *Awk!* What *happened* to them? I can't play Lou Reed that way! [*he straightens out the sunglasses and puts them on*]

"I can dig it. [*pause*] Yeah, right, right. [*pause*] Leather shirts, *right*, right. [*long pause*] Four-year-old boy? Far *out*. I can get behind… I know where you're coming from. Oh, we're back on the air?"

"Well, Lou, what is this about perversion in your life?"

And I'm saying, "What the fuck you *talking* about, man? Y'know, I didn't do nothing."

"Can we go back on that one? Lou…no cursing. Right, brother?"

Get a hippie handshake and a little goose under the table. I don't believe where this cat is *coming* from. Okay, back to Lou Reed.

"Lou…tell us about your faggot friends."

"Now, *wait* a minute, man. You didn't say we were discussing that. If you want to get into politics, the way I feel about the platform of the Democratic party—"

"Cut! You can't do that, man. Do you turn on, by the way?"

"Are we *on* now?" Like, he's got me going. Turn on to *who*? He means *what*? This is behind the scenes, under the table. What am I going to do? They said, "Be nice to him, he's the Program Director." But he's got his *hand* on my leg! *Really*. Suppose *you're* doing an interview with somebody and you suddenly feel *paw, paw, paw*. Slurping sounds and you're wearing headphones. Is he breathing loudly or is it me? It's not me, it's my—

[*abruptly stops to look at his watch*] I'll take my pulse and see if I'm alive. That's why I have my stopwatch, see? It's happening again, see? Ah *hah!*

MORGAN: How often do you have to check?

REED: Huh? Every five seconds.

MORGAN: Every five seconds?

REED: Yeah.

MORGAN: You missed the last hour, you'll have to do double time.

REED: No, the watch only works if I walk, and I haven't walked in years.

MORGAN: Oh, a pedometer?

REED: No, I take the bus. I'm in favor of bussing. Not to schools, though. I want *them* to mix with *me*.

MORGAN: When are you gonna run for President?

REED: Jimmy Carter really interests me. 'Cause I saw him last night on this TV… [*looking at his twisted sunglasses*] I can't believe I did that to my beautiful air flight, make believe… These are Japanese, they cost five bucks. They look like Ray Bans that cost thirty. Very hip. As long as you don't twist them out of shape. [*puts on his sunglasses*] Is that hip? *Dig it, man*. I can get instantly hostile and sinister this way.

MORGAN: It's a defence mechanism.

REED: [*suddenly yelling*] YEEEEEAH!!! That's a defence mechanism. I'll just slip into my…*thing*. Dig it, baby. Go ahead. *Dig* yourself.

MORGAN: What's all this about perversion in your latest album, Lou?

REED: [*bangs table loudly and mutters to himself theatrically*]

MORGAN: Hey, your nails aren't black! And what happened to the blonde hair? And—

REED: That's what a little kid said to me yesterday. We ran him over. His dyed hair was *running*. Oh, it was so *embarrassing*. A little sixteen year old twit. There was a mob of screaming kids, about four of them. With a leader. And his hair was dyed black and he had the black fingernails and the whole thing. It was so embarrassing 'cause when he *turned*, the dye was running; he must've used shoe polish. I wanted to know why his tongue wasn't black. You gotta do the whole thing, kid. Tongue niggers, y'know, in the street. Lou was racist on top of everything.

It's that or two hot pencils up your nose. A steaming hot pin up your pops. That's an image that occurs continually. That's an old…that's a Henny Youngman joke. You wanna hear a Henny Youngman joke?

MORGAN: Please.

REED: A traveling salesman's on the road and he's getting really fucking horny, right?

Okay, I love that, y'know, all rock has done for me is given me an audience for my bad jokes.

And he's just getting really hot to trot. So he goes into this gasoline station and he runs into the men's room. And, like, there's a *hole in the wall* about the size of a quarter, and it *takes* a quarter,

and says: "Your Home Away From Home." He figures, *fantastic*. And he whips it out, puts it in, puts in the quarter. And you hear this gnashing of gears and this…just this awful pain, and he's trying to pull it out and he *can't* get it out. And it's just excruciating. *Finally* the machine stops and he pulls his cock out…and it's got a little button sewn on at the tip.

MORGAN: [*silence*]

REED: [*laughs*] Isn't that terrible? No? I got *another* one. [*laughs*] Try *this* one on for size. That's what, you know, famous, famous, traveling sa… I mean, that's a *really* gross joke. Wanna hear *another* one?

These guys are running around the Village.

It's joke time.

Running around and they can't get laid. So they're *so* horny they finally see this nigger with a *really* beastial nose, y'know. Bestial nose. Large nostrils. And they say, "Can we fuck you up the nose, five bucks each." He says: [*grunts in an African voice*]. So they go and they fuck him up the nose, a nostril each. So they say, "*It's not bad.*" You know, they're pulling out. And then, y'know, give the guy five bucks, guy looks at them, guy says: [*in an African voice*] "By the way, you got any *social diseases?*" They say, "No, why?" [*inhales deeply through his nose*]

MORGAN: [*withering silence*]

REED: No? I got *another* one. You said you wanted to hear Henny Youngman jokes.

MORGAN: About this definitive interview… I'll take a station identification break for a couple of jokes, all right? Tell one more, then.

REED: No. That's my favorite. Henny Youngman had a Dial-A-Joke.

MORGAN: What were the jokes like?

REED: *Fantastic*. If you like those kind. "Behind every great man there's a woman, nagging." That's another Henny Youngman joke. That wasn't mine. Those enough one liners? Enough to make you sad.

MORGAN: How much do you sit around, watching TV?

REED: I don't.

MORGAN: Where do you pick these up?

REED: Word of mouth. [*laughs*] See, this won't translate to the written page.

MORGAN: I'm going to put out a joke book.

REED: A thousand and one gags. All you do is, you give it a hot towel and

some tape. [laughs]

MORGAN: You'll laugh when you see these in National Lampoon next month.

REED: I'll apply for a job. [makes muffled gagged sounds] "Lemme talk, it's true!" [more muffled gagged sounds] "Where's Cheap Thrills, I'll prove my point. See? Isn't that funny? That's me, it's not him. It's not him!" [bangs table] "It's me! Fuck! Screwed again."

MORGAN: You're such a loveable character, I can't see why you get all this bad press. It's the Jerry Lewis lovability—

REED: It's the Dean Martin build that does it. Jerry Lewis has had more horrors than all of Hollywood combined. And, as a nation of horrors, we, who are supplicants ask—in resignation, if not denegation—why is it onomatopoetics has left us?

MORGAN: [very long silence]

REED: [laughs] Not impressed, huh?

MORGAN: [continued silence]

REED: Oh, well… The existential transmogrification of the soul, if not the body. An exegesis performed if not by will, against the will. If not by Roger, then by power. No? Okay. He was the guy, y'know. Will Rogers and Powers, who went over in the U2? Remember? Think back.

MORGAN: Great humorist.

REED: Oh yeah. Ahead of my time, if not out of my league.

MORGAN: You're getting there.

REED: But it's lonely and there's no company and I'm already… I'm at minus two. Y'know, imagine plus seven. "Hey, look at those guys! Gee, they're the giants of our intellect."

MORGAN: You're in the wrong vocation.

REED: No, I'm in an avocation, not a vocation; that's the difference.

MORGAN: Did you ever see—

REED: I can't see, I've been blind for four years! Why don't they print that?

MORGAN: Gosh, Stevie, why did you write "Superstition"?

REED: That's why I like National Lampoon; when they had that special issue when they had Stevie Wonder on the cover with the 3D glasses? I love it. Is that tasteless or is that tasteless? Aren't they hip? They got it together.

MORGAN: Speaking of tasteless, have you read the Hendrix interview in the new CREEM?

REED: Yeeeah… [pause] No. I mean, I've seen it. I know that it's there, but I can't bring myself to read it.

MORGAN: I thought Ronson was supposed to be producing your new album.

REED: Eddie Fisher is being flown in to produce my new album, with Richard Burton as subcontractor. Burton, when asked about his first production facilities, said: [in Burton's voice] "Yes, Liz and I have talked and we're getting Lou the best Negroes available from our huge warehouse out on Sunset Strip. Get me a Negro!"

"Lou, you seem hung up on the black side of the wild side, is that true?"

"I'm into funk if that's [sniffs theatrically] what you mean." [laughs]

MORGAN: Who are your favorite comedians?

REED: Fields, obviously. Groucho. Mae West. And a guy I saw on TV the other night, Steve Martin.

MORGAN: Red Skelton?

REED: No way.

MORGAN: What's wrong with Red Skelton?

REED: [affronted] He's drunk. I think George Burns is great.

"Gracie, tell me…"

"Oh, no!"

"Say goodnight, Gracie."

MORGAN: Goodnight, Lou.

☆☆☆

PART SEVEN: ONE MORE TIME

☆☆☆

MORGAN: I hope you don't expect me to tell you how great Rock And Roll Heart is, 'cause I haven't got a copy.

REED: You know I couldn't expect anybody to compliment me. You know how disappointed I'd be.

MORGAN: Well, any man who can write a line like: "I see my life before me as a seamstress sees her pins" … that man has got to have something there.

REED: Now where did you ever get to see that? How did you get to see that?

MORGAN: "We Are The People."

REED: How did you get to see that?

MORGAN: "A Very Pure And Old-Fashioned Christmas."

REED: How in hell's name did you ever get to see any of those?

MORGAN: Where there's a will, there's a way.

REED: Hmmm…

MORGAN: Are there any copies of "We Are The People" around?

REED: It's gone.

MORGAN: Does it exist in any forms? Xerox or mimeograph?

REED: I don't have a copy. Like, I was gonna have a book published and I was looking around for that poem and I couldn't find it.

MORGAN: Well, if you still need it…

REED: No, that's what's so funny. That's when Bob Somma had Fusion. That was a great poem. That was terrific but I don't have a copy of it. Oh, that poem "We Are The People," that's such a great poem. Y'know, I can't remember it all.

MORGAN: There's a lot of Walt Whitman in it.

REED: I'm honestly not that familiar with Walt Whitman.

MORGAN: The two styles are very similar. They're the kind of poems that need to be read out loud.

REED: Oh, see like, I do that all the time with Anne Waldman, y'know. The Saint Lawrence Church on the Bowery. Anne single-handedly created that whole—well, you've heard of it…the poetry centers. The Saint Lawrence Church. Well, she created that. That wasn't always there. She had a thing called Another World. She used to edit it. She's had books of poetry and created that whole thing. Y'know, poetry workshops. And every year there's a reading. The last one was like, last January. Like, I was there and John was there. I mean, everybody was there. We were doing that with Anne before anybody was anybody. Like, if Anne hadn't gotten in touch with me to be in it, I'd've been really hurt.

MORGAN: Using a church like that is brilliant. Just for the atmosphere alone…

REED: Oh, yeah.

MORGAN: So how come it's taken you so long to get back on the road?

REED: There's a reason why the show that was supposed to be around last time was cancelled.

MORGAN: Yeah, what's the story on that? You were originally booked to come in last April. What happened?

REED: I didn't want to do it.

MORGAN: C'mon, aren't you going to give me something meatier than that?

REED: New management agency, new record company, it's not hard to figure out. I'm in litigation, I'm still—

MORGAN: Tied up, eh?

REED: No. *Oh*, no. No, there is justice in this world. Of course, you have to be… I mean, this has been going on almost a year and a half, man. They figure, though, they can wear you down financially, spiritually, mentally. Waiting for you to fall.

MORGAN: But you're not.

REED: I mean, to the point where just out of *perversity* I won't. 'Cause on a certain level, and I think you can understand it, you'd just like to walk away from it and say: "Fuck it." Not only is it not *worth* it, but who *needs* it? I'm gonna massacre 'em. It's so dirty and so fuckin' scummy. They underestimated me. I'm gonna *kill* 'em.

MORGAN: Did they think they were dealing with a dummy?

REED: I'm a very patient person. I'm a very *vengeful* person. Y'know, I can wait forever to get back. Really. I'm not about to wait for the time when they say: "Let's settle."

MORGAN: Time heals all wounds.

REED: There's no wound and there's no time to heal anything. I'll sit around until I'm seventy-five to see this thing down. I don't care. They didn't bank on that. The day before the tour I was in a deposition where they had me… Y'know, the enemy lawyer gets to work you over. Seven straight hours. And they have eight lawyers. Me and my lawyer and eight of them. Eight. *Eight!* Eight, y'know, representing different—

MORGAN: Facets of the… Yeah, I can imagine. That alone would be enough to intimidate you.

REED: Yeah. Well, they figure you've gotta fall 'cause you're under pressure. You've got to survive monetarily. Y'know, make a record. How can you make a record and go on tour with this and that—

MORGAN: With all that going down.

REED: Well, that's the idea. Plus, of course, it costs money to defend yourself on top of everything else. Like, these are heavy lawyers.

MORGAN: Well, what's going on? You're on Arista now, the Kinks are on Arista, Bowie's going to WEA—

REED: David can't get out. Y'know, *I* didn't think *I* could, either. I was six hundred thousand dollars in the red. It's dirty. Dirtier than anything you can conceive of. Really. I wouldn't want to tell you. I'm *in* it and it's hard for me to comprehend it. It's just a vicious, dirty…

MORGAN: When did you first see it coming?

REED: A long time ago. There was nothing I could do about it. Except keep my mouth shut and not blow it.

— **previously unpublished, 2021**

(complete unedited version, recorded in March 1976 and October 1976)

To Jeffrey! your friend Red Skelton

THE
WHO

PAUL McCARTNEY

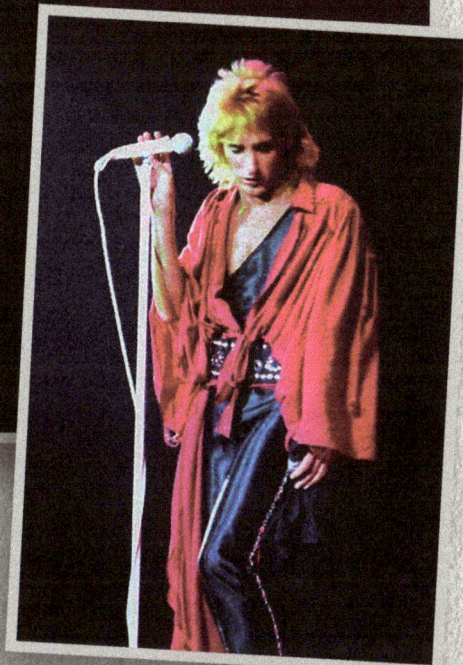

**ROD
STEWART**

This really happened, although not exactly as published. Dylan was walking away from the microphone when I said my piece, so he had to turn back to respond. As can be heard on several different bootlegged audience recordings of the concert, Dylan's actual reply to me was said with a laugh: "I dunno, man, I dunno!"

THE DIMINUTIVE BOB DYLAN INTERVIEW
by Machine Rock

The Guinness Book Of World Records has officially given credit for the world's shortest Bob Dylan interview to CREEM rock critic Jeffrey Morgan for the following exchange between Dylan (who was performing on stage during a recent Toronto concert) and Morgan (who was sitting in a front row center seat at the time):

DYLAN: This next number is a song I once did with The Band. You remember The Band, don't you? It was on an album called *Planet Waves*. It sold twelve copies.

MORGAN: *Why?*

DYLAN: Get this guy outta here.

Even though he missed the rest of the concert, Morgan later called the exchange "a great rock 'n' roll moment. Almost as good as the time I asked Lou Reed if he was scared of death."

Dylan was unavailable for comment.

— **CREEM, July 1979**

I, THE CRITIC

DAVID BOWIE
"Heroes"
(RCA)

I soon found out that she was no stranger to scotch and that she loved to dance. We closed the night club just before two and when we arrived back at my place she was still raring to go. I had a wicked deadline to meet in seven hours and was more than ready to call it a night, but it soon became evident that she had other designs.

My hand was slipping just inside her elastic when, suddenly, two men slid out of the bedroom closet. The pair didn't say anything, but I heard a click. One of them had a switchblade knife; the blade looked as long as a saber. I drop-kicked him in the groin and moved towards the other one who, by this time, was heading for the front door. He never made it. Lunging, I grabbed him by the collar, redirecting his head into the nearest well. Plaster and shattered cartilage massed into a pulpy smear as his bloodied face slid silently towards the plush carpet below.

Adjusting my tie, I turned towards Velma who was lying nude on the bed, looking infinitely desirable. Crossing the floor, I started to remove my jacket when my foot struck something that one of the thugs must have dropped. Bending over to pick it up, I saw that it was a record album. Unable to make out the lettering on the front cover, I switched on the bedroom light.

It was a Bowie album. A new one. The cover photograph intrigued me. Obviously, here was a man with a couple of screws loose. Turning, I entered the living room and switched on the stereo. Slipping Jackie Gleason's *Music For Lovers* back into its jacket, I used the discarded switchblade to slit the shrink-wrap on the Bowie disc.

As I placed it on the turntable, Velma came bounding out of the bedroom, still naked. She splayed herself suggestively on the couch. I considered showing her the album cover, but didn't. What Velma wanted from me was something far more urgent; already her undulations were beginning to soak a hole into the upholstery. Women.

I pushed the automatic start and waited. Instant on and out, the JBLs started spitting piano and drums. Writhing on the couch, Velma pretended not to notice the steady pulse punching out of the twin speakers, but I wasn't fooled. Already I could tell that this was Bowie's best album since *Hunky Dory* was released in December of 1971.

Good, strong voice. Besides, he was writing *songs* again, not just the quick tonal glimpses that characterized so much of *Low*. I was impressed all right. The title track alone told me that Bowie meant business by moving like heroin sound fragments merged with crashed car synthetexures. The mood inevitable through anonymous lower registers and stylistic high-changes. In fact, all of the first side was like that: a desperate urgency defined but without the obviousness of *Station To Station*. Almost as if it were recorded during *The Man Who Sold The World* sessions, but more advanced through experience.

The flip was a good flow, too. Kraftwerked tribute into thick chorded down scales with strings and Euro-atmospheres. The ghosts of birds passing through air elusive. An expanse of space...untested. Steady frame of reference: low-glow orange hum. A roar of sudden jets over the horizon: melancholy turn with Champion sax. New geography element introduced and complexity. Aural orientation: a search. Broken...disjointed...a lonely cry. Silence.

The circuits shut down with a solid click.

I looked over at the couch. Empty.

I shut the stereo off. Three in the morning. Six hours to the deadline. I could almost hear my editor now. She had the kind of voice that'd be erotic if it weren't so narcotic. Screw it. Take the phone off the hook and sleep in. It's only money. Money made from an aesthetic depression.

All my heroes are dead or dying.

— StageLife, November 1977

I first met William S. Burroughs in February 1974, at which time I asked him to autograph a photograph of himself standing next to David Bowie. As he signed his name in the available space over his head, Burroughs drawled: "You oughtta get Booey to sign the other half." When Booey showed up in town later that year on his Diamond Dogs *tour, I did just that.*

INSIDE WILLIAM BURROUGHS

With 1980 just a shot away, it seems as good a time as any for a cultural update from William S. Burroughs, the spiritual patriarch of rock 'n' roll.

The uninitiated may wonder why this magazine has devoted so much space to a man who will be 65 years old this year. Such readers are advised to pursue some of the man's previous books: *Junky* (written more than a quarter of a century ago under the pseudonym William Lee because Burroughs didn't want his family to read it), *Nova Express*, or *Exterminator!*, any of which will more than pave the way for Burroughs' acknowledged masterwork, *Naked Lunch*.

Of equal importance is *The Job*, a vital collection of interviews which will answer even the most avid reader's questions.

Still, despite the amount of topical ground *The Job* covers, precious little, if any, information concerning Burroughs' personal opinions on rock 'n' roll can be found in print—a situation I decided to remedy when I recently interviewed him.

JEFFREY MORGAN: For many contemporary rock critics and musicians, William Burroughs *is* rock 'n' roll. Do you feel the same affinity for rock 'n' roll that rock 'n' roll obviously feels for you?

WILLIAM S. BURROUGHS: Well, yeah. [*laughs*] I *have* given them a lot of titles: The Heavy Metal Kids, The Insect Trust, The Soft Machine…there are a couple of others.

I enjoy rock 'n' roll. It certainly is a unique and incredible phenomenon. Remember that 40 or 50 years ago, musicians didn't make any money. They played to very small audiences in night clubs and road houses. Also, they had no protection on their records.

I'm always asking rock 'n' roll people if they know who Petrillo is, and none of them do. Well, they wouldn't have a dime if it weren't for Petrillo because he organized the Musician's Union way back at the end of the '30s. And that is why they make money on their records. There wouldn't be any white Rolls Royces or anything like that.

MORGAN: Did Jimmy Page know who Petrillo was when you talked to him?

BURROUGHS: [*laughs*] No. I'll tell you one who *would* know is Mick Jagger. He's a businessman, he went to the London School Of Economics.

MORGAN: Can you see the intersection point between your works and rock 'n' roll?

BURROUGHS: Well, I think that, in a way, we're both—I mean, of course, they're operating in much more of a mass area, but the ideas are similar. Some of the content is similar: the drugs, et cetera. There are a number of places where we overlap.

MORGAN: Did you see *The Man Who Fell To Earth*?

BURROUGHS: Yes. I thought it had some very interesting sections. It wasn't bad, but I didn't think it was great, either.

MORGAN: What did you think of *Diamond Dogs*? Have you heard it?

BURROUGHS: Vaguely, yes. It's been a long time since I saw it, actually. Yeah, I thought that Bowie did quite a good job there. I just didn't think that the film overall had that much impact. I thought the alien aspect was conveyed very well.

MORGAN: No, no. Did you ever hear the *record* he made after you interviewed him in 1973? The one he made after reading half of *Nova Express*?

BURROUGHS: Oh, yeah, yeah. [*dryly*] That is fun.

MORGAN: What did you think of him when you met him? Did he seem to be the kind of guy who was bullshitting his way through life or did he seem to be walking the straight and narrow?

BURROUGHS: [*laughs*] Well, neither one. He's not bullshitting, he's very, very clever and I think very calculating. I think he knows exactly what he's doing and where he's going and how to get there.

MORGAN: How is *Junky*, the motion picture, progressing?

BURROUGHS: On again, off again. No Hollywood project is on until it's on screen and it's never completely dead until the whole film industry is dead. Many scripts have been battered around Hollywood as long as ten years, so I won't say it's dead. We have a script and people have expressed interest, so it may work out.

We talked an awful lot about whether *Junky* should be shot as a contemporary film in a contemporary setting, and I said absolutely not. The reason is very simple because the whole junk scene has changed so unrecognizably since that time that, if you start shooting it in 1970, you might as well throw the book away and do another script.

As far as box office is concerned, it's not very good box office. They don't want to see people sticking needles in their arms.

MORGAN: How did Patti Smith get involved in the filming of *Junky*?

BURROUGHS: Well, she simply said that she'd like to play a part if the film was produced.

MORGAN: What is there about her poetry that you like—if anything.

BURROUGHS: Well, she is good as a performer. It isn't the poetry itself, it's the way she puts it across. She's a terrific performer, a great stage presence. To read the poetry doesn't mean that much to me, but to see her perform it—the energy that she generates is really something.

MORGAN: So you don't care for her poetry on the printed page then.

BURROUGHS: No. It's something that's made to be performed, it seems to me.

MORGAN: Your long-awaited new book, *Cities Of The Red Night*, is scheduled for release later this year and, at over 700 pages, it's going to be your longest book yet. Can you tell us something about it?

BURROUGHS: It's got a very different plot to it. Plots and sub-plots. It's very much a romantic play with trick endings and so on—so for that reason, I don't talk too much about it. I don't want to give away the ending. [*laughter*]

MORGAN: Is there any advice you'd like to give to young writers?

BURROUGHS: I have an exercise I learned from a Mafia Don in Ohio: see everybody on the street before they see you. It's quite interesting actually because, if you see everyone before they see you, they won't see you.

And then you'll find that somebody beat you.

— CREEM, March 1979

I began writing the following record review on the evening of Sunday July 27th, several hours before Bob Hope's death later that night. After much soul-searching, I decided to finish the review as a tribute to Mr. Hope. I also decided to finish the review because I'd started writing it while Mr. Hope was still alive. But mainly I decided to finish the review because I couldn't come up with another idea.

THE ROAD TO HEAVEN

THE FONDAS
Coming Now!
(SFTRI)

FADE IN.

VOICE OVER: The following program is brought to you in living color on NBC.

ANNOUNCER: Live from North Korea, it's "Bob Hope's One Hundredth Birthday Bash" with Brooke Shields, Ann Margaret, Ann Jillian, Phyllis Diller, and special musical guests The Fondas! And now the star of our show, Bob Hope!

[*"Thanks For The Memories" plays as Hope walks out jauntily with a golf club slung over his shoulder.*]

HOPE: Yeah! Thank you! Thank you very much! This is Bob "Seoul Brother Number One" Hope coming to you live from P'yŏngyang, North Korea. P'yŏngyang. That's Korean for "Badges? We don't need no stinkin' badges." But seriously, I wanna thank President Kim Jong Il for letting me into the country to try one of his nuclear tanning booths. They wheeled me in and half an hour later I walked out a new man. Boy, I wanna tell ya, ain't that somethin'? I haven't felt this good since Dorothy Lamour—

VOICE: Uh-uh, now don't you go tellin' tales out of school, Junior…

[*Bing Crosby walks out to a standing ovation.*]

HOPE: Bing Crosby! What are *you* doing here in P'yŏngyang, North Korea? I thought you were dead!

CROSBY: [*puffing on pipe*] Radiation, buddy boy, radiation. It's not just for centenarians anymore.

HOPE: Still smoking, huh? I *told* you that stuff would kill you.

CROSBY: Ah, you're a funny boy, funny boy. You mean to say I've been gone all these years and they *still* haven't found a cure for the greatest killer known to man?

HOPE: What, cancer?

CROSBY: No, your jokes.

HOPE: Well, I… [*does double take*] Well, I have to admit you're looking pretty chipper for an old man of… *How* many centuries is it now?

CROSBY: Well, if the truth be told, Der Bingle will *also* be one hundred years young later this year. [*touching Hope's lapels*] And I must say, *you've* got a certain glow about yourself as well. Even if it *is* green.

HOPE: [*brushing Crosby's hand away*] Hey, don't kid yourself, that's not radioactivity: I just ate at the NBC commissary.

CROSBY: [*laughing*] Ah! So what's the birthday boy have on tap for the evening's festivities?

HOPE: Oh, we've got a *great* show lined up for tonight.

CROSBY: Do tell, do tell!

HOPE: Well, we've got the lovely and talented Brooke Shields! The beautiful Ann Margaret! The exquisite Ann Jillian! America's favorite funny lady, Phyllis Diller! Plus of course, Les Brown and his Band of Renown! And now to get things started, here are two of my favorite actors performing together musically for the very first time, Jane and Peter Fonda!

[*The Fondas perform "Wanna Be." As the song ends, the Korean Guard howl and wolf whistle while singer Julie Benjamin adjusts her tight tube top.*]

HOPE: Hey, *wait* a minute! That's not Hanoi Jane!

CROSBY: Of course not, Junior. Those kids are Detroit's number one garage band, the fabulous Fondas.

And they just performed a track from their new album *Coming Now!*

HOPE: What do *you* know about today's modern music? The last time you had a hit record it was released on an Edison wax cylinder.

CROSBY: Why, the old groaner's been championing fresh new talent all his life. Don't tell me you've forgotten my swingin' swansong duet with David Bowie? I hear that lad has turned into quite the avant garde artiste.

HOPE: Say, who died and made *you* Lester Bangs?

CROSBY: Why it's sacrilege to even *suggest* such a thing, Junior. But now that you mention it, you may be interested to know that I actually spoke to the great man before I got here.

HOPE: You did? Well, what did he say? Did he wish me a happy birthday?

CROSBY: No, but he did want me to spread the good word on his behalf.

HOPE: On his behalf?

CROSBY: He would've come down himself but he's a very busy boy these days, very busy. And so I'm here at his behest.

HOPE: Busy with what?

CROSBY: Why, his blurtin' band, Junior! You see, The Bangs-Laughner Experience is so busy packing them in upstairs at the Silver Lining that he sent me down to tell the world that, in his opinion, these here Fondas have definitely got what it takes.

Lester says that they've got the dirty distortion smarts of the Leaves, the sexy hubba hubba come-hither charm of the early Debbie Blondie, and that they're the perfect *Shindig-Hullabaloo* white go go boot feel good antidote for everything that's wrong with the world today.

Also, in Lester's opinion, any band that

can squeeze fourteen songs onto an album that's only thirty-five minutes long is beating the Ramones at their own game! Not to mention the fact that he'd rather look at lungstress Julie Benjamin than distressed Joey Ramone any day.

HOPE: [*looking over*] Boy, you're not kidding. She makes Raquel Welch look like an ironing board that was run over by a steamroller, doesn't she? I haven't seen a set of dishes stacked that high since I starred with Jane Russell in *The Paleface* and she—

CROSBY: *Uh-uh*, Junior. Be nice or I won't give you your birthday present.

HOPE: [*excited*] You got me a present?

CROSBY: Absolutely! I brought along a very good friend.

HOPE: You did?

CROSBY: Only one of the most caustic commentators of all time!

HOPE: Does he have a wicked sense of humor?

CROSBY: Most certainly!

HOPE: And a big mustache?

CROSBY: Indeed he does!

HOPE: And you said Lester was too busy on the road to Heaven to show up!

CROSBY: Ah, you're a smart one, Junior. I knew I couldn't pull a fast one on you!

HOPE: [*laughing*] On me? Are you kidding? Trying to sneak America's Greatest Rock Critic by America's Greatest Comedian is like trying to sneak sunrise past a rooster! Well, where *is* he? Where *is* the great man?

VOICE: *Ahhhhhhhhhh!* Hope!

[*Jerry Colonna walks out to a standing ovation.*]

HOPE: Jerry Colonna! What are *you* doing here in P'yŏngyang, North Korea?

COLONNA: [*twirling his mustache*] I'm here to pick up my date, Hope!

HOPE: Your date?

JULIE: Ready, tiger?

COLONNA: *Ahhhhhhhhhh!*

JULIE: [*winking*] Bye, boys!

CROSBY: [*watching them slowly stroll off*] Make sure she's home by eleven, son.

HOPE: Boy, can you *believe* the nerve of that guy? Coming back from the dead and stealing my girl like that?

CROSBY: Stealing *your* girl? After *I* saw her first? Why, *you* thought she was Jane Fonda!

HOPE: Hey, you can't talk about my girl like that!

COLONNA: [*turning around*] Say, Hope!

HOPE: Yeah, Jerry?

COLONNA: [*eyes bulging*] Thanks for the mammaries!

ANNOUNCER: Stay tuned! Bob will be right back after these words from Chrysler and Pepsodent!

APPLAUSE AND FADE OUT.

— **CREEM, July 2003**

Julie Benjamin Photograph © Robert Matheu

**IAN HUNTER
AND
MICK
RONSON**

Several months after Bat Out Of Hell was released, I had the pleasure of speaking with the two comedic cut-ups responsible for what remains to this day one of the biggest selling classic rock albums of all time. Not that you'd ever know it from our cavalier conversation, during which time none of us mentioned the record even once.

IS MEAT LOAF THE ORSON WELLES OF ROCK?

Riding up the hotel elevator, mere minutes away from a face-to-face confrontation with the (you'd better believe it) one and only Meat Loaf, I've got this stupid Henny Youngman joke ricocheting around in my brain and I just can't seem to shake it out: "My wife is so fat that when she sits around the house, *she really sits around the house*..." Now considering the sheer physical girth of critical mass that comprises The Loaf, clearly this is not a joke that one would recount in his presence—at least, not out loud.

☆☆☆

Y'see, Meat Loaf isn't *fat* so much as he's just...well, slightly *overweight*. I mean, when you usually think of a fat person, inevitably a picture comes to mind of a being somewhat akin to a sluggish, flab-layered jelly donut, incapable of even the most simplistic of motor activities. Meat Loaf, on the other hand, has the kind of natural power presence which indicates that, if he so desired, he could destroy you into a pulpy mess using only the pinky finger of his left hand.

In fact, the only other person who could even come *close* to matching the above description would be Orson Welles. Indeed, after watching The Loaf command the El Mocambo stage for two nights last month, I was awed by the fact that if Orson Welles of *Citizen Kane* (i.e., POWER) ever merged with the Orson Welles of *Touch Of Evil* (i.e., SIZE) and formed a rock 'n' roll band, he'd be Meat Loaf.

"Yeah, a few people have mentioned that," says Jim Steinman, Meat Loaf's pianist and principle composer (not to mention Joseph Cotton foil.) "*Touch Of Evil* is my favorite," he continues. "The great thing about Orson Welles is the combination of power and brilliance. I really identify with Orson Welles, too. I mean, he's my favorite film director. He and Hitchcock. *Touch Of Evil* and *Psycho* are my favorite movies, too. I've seen both of them twenty times. You can't top anything in movies for Orson Welles' entrance in *Touch Of Evil*, coming out of that car."

☆☆☆

At this point, Meat Loaf (who up until now had been conducting another interview in the bathroom, of all places) emerged into the room like a wild panther stalking his prey. Eyes wild and long blond hair flying back, The Loaf looked as if he had just eaten Ted Nugent for breakfast.

"Boy, is it ever hard trying to be Jim Steinman and Meat Loaf at the same time," he growled at me, referring to the one-man bathroom interview. "What's all this about me being the Orson Welles of rock?" he demanded. He had heard the comparisons before, I gathered. "*Orson Welles*...yeah," he admitted in a low tone.

After all, when he's performing, Meat Loaf sure looks the part, storming all over the stage as if he owned it—

"I *DO* OWN IT!" he bellowed in a voice that almost shattered the windows. "As far as I'm concerned, it's *mine*," he glared.

I mentioned that it was great to hear a vocalist who can hit the same notes on stage that he does on the record.

"Yeah, I *work* at makin' it," explained The Loaf.

"My auditions are like athletic events," confides Steinman, a full moon playing lightly on his shoulders. "When I was doing theater and I was auditioning singers for musicals, all I'd ever say was 'could you do that louder and could you raise it five steps?' I just can't stand hearing a singer singing comfortably."

"He never asked *me* to do that, though," says The Loaf smugly.

"But the habit's always been with Meat to end up on a hospital bed, having sung five nights in a row," counters Steinman. " 'Do you think we could lower the key a bit?' " says Steinman, impersonating The Loaf.

Would he ever *do* such a thing to help out his partner's throat?

"ABSOLUTELY NOT! It'll sound great—even if you're *bleeding*. I think it's thrilling even if your voice is *ripped up*..."

☆☆☆

Suddenly I'm aware of a faint scratching outside the hotel room door. I ignore it and shift uneasily in my chair.

"I'm a big fan of German opera," Steinman continues. "I grew up loving Wagner—"

"I CAN'T *STAND* OPERA!" screams The Loaf in a furry of obscene denunciations.

"Meat's not into opera, is he?" I ask Steinman.

"Uh, no...he's not *into* it...he's not a real opera freak...but we're both *sports* freaks..."

At last! A topic I can sink my teeth into! "Oh yeah?" I crow. "Whaddya into? What kind of sports? Hockey? Baseball?

"Baseball, man, baseball!" screams The Loaf, the blood rushing to his brain.

"Baseball," agrees Steinman. "Baseball's beautiful."

"Didja follow Oakland a couple of years ago?" I ask. "Campy Campaneris—"

"Nah, I'm a *Yankee* fan," asserts Meat.

"I was a *Mets* fan," confesses Steinman. "I love baseball more than anything. Football is, like, chaos." Suddenly Steinman's eyes glaze over, trance-like. He leans towards me, his voice a menacing monotone of suppressed passion. "The beauty of baseball is that it's...*infinite*..."

☆☆☆

The scratching outside the door becomes more pronounced; a thick gray mist starts wrapping itself around my ankles.

"A baseball inning could go on, theoretically, *forever*..."

"But what's this got to do with your *music?*" I scream, bolting out of the room and down the hall towards the elevator.

Just as the doors open in front of me, I can hear Steinman screaming: "IF FOOTBALL IS LED ZEPPELIN, THE GREATEST THING ABOUT BASEBALL IS THAT IT'S THE BEACH BOYS!"

Adjusting the garland of wolfsbane around my neck, I push the button marked 'lobby' and prepare myself for the slow descent down.

— StageLife, February 1978

40 MINUTES

PHIL COLLINS
No Jacket Required
(Atlantic)

FADE IN.

MIKE WALLACE: And now, a few minutes with Andy Rooney.

ANDY ROONEY: My 14-year-old niece had a birthday last week. I wanted to give her a few dollars but her family said, no, what she'd really like is a new record for her stereo, so I went to the neighborhood record store. Record stores sure have changed since when I was a kid, so I asked a salesman to show me some new releases.

The first one he showed me was something called *VU* by The Velvet Underground. I'd never heard of them, but the salesman said they were famous for songs like "Heroin" "Venus to Furs." That didn't seem like the thing for a 14-year-old girl, so I asked to see something else.

The salesman showed me *She's The Boss*, the new Mick Jagger LP. I passed on that one, too. The last time Mick Jagger recorded without The Rolling Stones, it was in *Performance*, and I don't think a 14-year-old girl should be exposed to something like that, either.

Then I spotted this old, balding guy. Looks like me, I thought. The salesman told me it was Phil Collins. Not the guy who sings for Genesis? Yes, the same guy. I'd been hooked on Phil's work ever since I heard "In The Air Tonight" on *Miami Vice*, so I asked the salesman to play me a few songs.

The opener, "Sussudio," ripped off the intro to Prince's "1999" and was way too loud for my liking. Come to think of it, so were "Only You Know And I know," "Don't Lose My Number," "Who Said I Would," and "I Don't Wanna Know." I liked the ballads better: "Take Me Home," "Long Way To Go," and the first single, "One More Night."

I asked the salesman why the album was called *No Jacket Required* since it not only came with a jacket, but with an inner sleeve as well. He didn't know the answer to that.

I also asked him why the back cover was an enlargement of Phil's forehead from the front cover. He didn't know the answer to that one either, but he assured me that *No Jacket Required* was the perfect gift for a 14-year-old girl. He told me that Phil Collins is hot, trendy, and commercial. He warned me, however, that *No Jacket Required* sounded just like *Face Values* and *Hello, I Must Be Going*, Phil's two previous albums.

I told him that since my 14-year-old niece didn't own any Phil Collins albums, that wouldn't be a problem. I thanked him for his help, bought the record, and gave it to my niece.

She took it back to the record store the next day and traded it in for a Motörhead LP.

Next year, I'm going to give her a sawbuck for her birthday and to hell with what her family says.

FADE OUT.

— CREEM, June 1985

PATTI SMITH

E STREET BAND

For those of you keeping score at home, this was my first rock 'n' roll interview.

TIME MACHINE SLUMMING IN THE NEGATIVE ZONE WITH KISS

Like many a person— perhaps even yourself—I was raised on a high decibel diet of rock music, comic books, and monster movies. And while all three genres have always been intrinsically intertwined, never were they so unified as in the '70s when every rock star in every musical genre from cocaine disco funk to country glitter punk looked as if he or she had stepped out of either a superhero comic or a superstitious cemetery.

So it made perfect perverse sense when a fledgling band embodying all three of these characteristics called KISS came to Toronto on September 14th 1974 to play a venue that officially went by the name of the Victory Theatre. This was a genteel way of referring to the venerable Victory Burlesque, a storied strip emporium where illustrious cleavage heavers such as Alexandra The Great 48 would regularly strut their stuff down the long center runway which bisected the seats some 10 rows deep.

KISS performed there twice that Saturday night—the 64th and 65th shows of their first ever tour in support of their self-titled debut album. After the first show was over, I flashed my homemade press pass and went backstage where

road manager Junior Smalling pointed me in the general direction of Paul Stanley and Gene Simmons, both of whom were idly loitering without intent.

JEFFREY MORGAN: Welcome back to Toronto! The first time you guys were here was three months ago in June when you played Massey Hall with the New York Dolls.

GENE SIMMONS: [looking over] The Dolls were with us.

MORGAN: Well, what do you think of this place?

PAUL STANLEY: [slowly nodding to himself] Oh, it's great. Really. I love this place. It's got atmosphere. It's—

MORGAN: Conducive to playing?

STANLEY: Yeah, exactly. That's it.

MORGAN: It's the last burlesque house left in Canada.

STANLEY: Yeah? That's great!

MORGAN: But this is a strip joint, and everybody knows that strip joints are representative of decadence incarnate. So are you trying to tell me that this place has it over Max's or the Academy?

STANLEY: Well, I mean, Max's is so small, you know… And the Academy's got ramps like this as well, it's only that this place is so much smaller—which is alright 'cause it all adds to the atmosphere of the place.

MORGAN: Yesterday I had a chat with a local promoter who said that although this is a great place for heavy metal

death bands to play, it sucked when it came to lightweight acts like Ry Cooder, who played here earlier in the year and died. It was his contention that the same people who would go out of their way to see someone like Cooder at a high class concert hall wouldn't go across the street to see him—and risk being seen—at a peeler palace like this.

STANLEY: [shaking his head] Gee, I really can't see that. I can't see what a place—or what a place looks like—has to do with people coming to see somebody. I just don't understand that.

MORGAN: Well, you're not going to deny that this place isn't broken down.

STANLEY: Broken down? [laughing] It's just broken, period.

JUNIOR SMALLING: [walking by] The stage isn't even big enough for us to hang our electric logo.

MORGAN: Gimme a one word description for this place.

SMALLING: One word…for this place? [spreads his arms wide to encompass the entire stage] Do I have to say it?

MORGAN: Tell me, is there any difference between playing this place and playing somewhere else? Don'tcha have to psyche yourself up or something like that to handle it?

SIMMONS: No, not at all. You see, what we're doing is essentially the same thing that strippers do.

MORGAN: It is, huh?

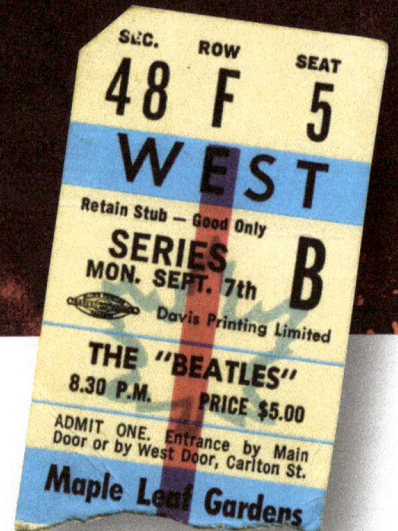

SIMMONS: Well, look at it this way. It's my belief that all of us are made of different distinct personalities. I firmly believe that you cannot show me a person and tell me that you know everything, every aspect about them. You just can't. It's impossible. Like, when I'm talking to you right now like this, I'm talking differently than if I were talking to my mother. And when I'm out there on stage, again I'm acting rather, er, *different*.

And it's the same with a stripper. When a stripper goes shopping, she goes shopping like everyone else. She doesn't go down the aisles going like this: [*moves his right hand around in a sash swinging style*]. So what we're doing is performing just like strippers do, if you understand what I mean.

MORGAN: Okay, but what about rock 'n' roll itself? Now me, I've been going to rock 'n' roll shows for ten years and—

SIMMONS: [*stunned*] Ten years?

MORGAN: Yeah, I started out with The Beatles back in '64.

SIMMONS: Y'know, you're lucky. That's the one thing I've always regretted.

MORGAN: What, you mean not having ever seen The Beatles?

SIMMONS: [*wistfully*] Yeah…

MORGAN: Well, that's understandable. I mean, you guys manage to come off on stage looking like a future mutant version of them. You've got the same visual structure and instruments, the same—

SIMMONS: Well, I've always liked them and I've never made any excuses for it.

MORGAN: I also notice a whole bunch of *other* influences thrown in as well, like Disney—

SIMMONS: Yeah, *Fantasia*, right? I just *love* movies, all *kinds* of them. *The Exorcist, Pink Flamingoes*…

MORGAN: Marvel Comics?

SIMMONS: [*beaming*] Yeah, especially!

(Suddenly I'm dimly aware that we're surrounded by several rummy groupies as well as KISS members Peter Criss and Ace Frehley. Simmons, blissfully oblivious to the buxom bottle peroxide blonde leaning heavily on his shoulder, continues to rave on with a wild gleam in his eye and all the zealous fervor of a true pop culture fanatic.)

SIMMONS: Y'know, I once had a fanzine that Neal Adams used to draw for! Name any superhero! C'mon! Name him and I'll tell you everything about him!

MORGAN: [*warily*] Okay… Spider-Man.

SIMMONS: Created in the early '60s by Stan Lee and Steve Ditko, who used to draw the Blue Beatle for Charlton. Debuted in *Amazing Fantasy* number fifteen and—

MORGAN: Alright, alright, you can stop now, you've convinced me.

SIMMONS: What was the first vampire movie?

MORGAN: *Nosferatu*.

SIMMONS: [*impressed*] *Nosferatu*, right! Made in Germany with Max Schreck and directed by—

PEROXIDE BLONDE: What about Captain Marvel?

SIMMONS: [*quickly turning on her*] Which one? Do you mean the Captain Marvel of the '30s or the later one?

(As Simmons went into a detailed thesis-length dissertation on both the Fawcett Captain Marvel as well as the Marvel Comics version, I took the opportunity to discreetly slip out the side door.)

— **Cheap Thrills, April 1976**

PASSION IS NO ORDINARY WORD

LYDIA LUNCH
13:13
(Ruby)

In a business where women singers are a dime a dozen these days (and trite women singers the norm), Lydia Lunch can be proud of being one of the few women singers in rock who consistently breaks the mold of complacency surrounding much of today's music and redefines the role of what a contemporary women in rock 'n' roll should be today, simply by doing what she wants, when she wants, and how she wants.

That she isn't cleaning up in any money or popularity sweepstakes (yet) is by no means indicative of any failure on her part. Let us not forget that, first and foremost, rock 'n' roll has always been about getting the music out of the mind of the creator and into the mind of the listener.

That Lydia continues to do just that, by recording and releasing albums on a steady basis, is not a commentary on how low the industry's standards have declined. On the contrary, the very existence of *13.13*, like all previous Lydia Lunch albums (not to mention a hell of a lot of other,

lesser known so-called "new music") is an affirmation that rock 'n' roll is still alive as a revolutionary force—not matter *what* some people may try to do to kill it.

Rock 'n' roll has also always been about passion—and Lydia Lunch has enough raw passion burning in her soul to recreate your lifetime several times over (or destroy it, if need be).

That it takes an artist like Lydia Lunch to open our eyes and make us see just exactly how emotionally artificial and shallow some of our major women singer/songwriters *really* are (and probably always were), is a sad commentary on how easy it's become for us to accept whatever watered-down opiate is shoved in front of us these days, rather than opt instead for the real thing—no matter how elusive it may be to find, and no matter how unattractive it may initially seem to be.

And although *13.13* is old news to Lydia Lunch by now, like all great music, it's still significantly different enough to make any "progressive" radio station playing "new music" blanch and (hopefully) recognize just exactly what kind of watered down, assembly line pap it's shoveling out to the kids of today.

Just as radio never played the Velvets, Stooges, or Dolls (and probably never will, although it does take perverse, ironic pride in programming the latest releases by Lou Reed, Iggy Pop, and David Johansen), likewise will radio never play Lydia Lunch regardless of whatever setting her music happens to be in. So if you want to hear this album, you're going to have to make the supreme effort of *actually going out and buying it* because you're never going to hear it otherwise.

Sure I could tell you about it but, believe me, whatever information I could impart to you about *13.13 still* wouldn't prepare you for any of Lydia Lunch's other previous musical excursions—which stylistically run the gamut from pure white-out noise to black *noir* R&B to languid torch 'n' speed-bop to the dark metal tome that is *13.13*.

And because every other Lydia Lunch album is so radically different from all her others, and because there is no easy solution to the dilemma of how to initially approach her music, my advice to you would be to simply have faith, pick a genre, and jump in. Faith, and a renewed belief in the future of rock 'n' roll and what you can do to be a part of it.

— CREEM, November 1982

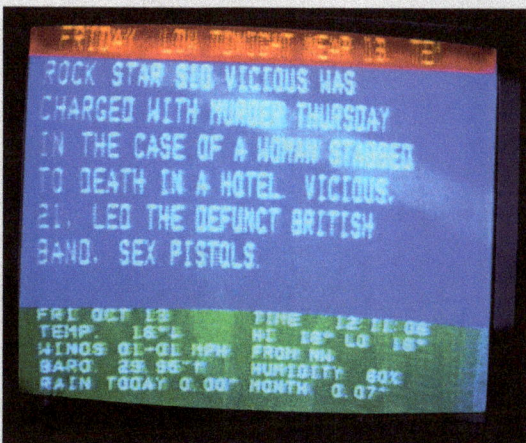

My earliest encounter with the eerily eternal entity known as *Nash The Slash* was in 1978, shortly after the release of his inaugural unaccompanied offering, Bedside Companion—a mere month before the life-altering auditory accident whose lashed but unleashed quadracane slawsonics would forever cause him to mask his mien.

That we immediately hit it off as slightly skewed kindred spirits was made manifest when Nash dedicated his Cut-Throat record label to me. When I wasn't amusing myself by etching ghastly engravings of the new veneered Nash—which often munificently ended up either in his magazine The Nashional Enquirer; on a concert poster; as a postcard; or projected onto a screen during a live performance—I was writing about him in CREEM, commencing with "Dial S For Slasher" in the May 1980 issue.

What follows is a mangled amalgamation of disinterred dissertations with a few new words grafted on here and there, all shoddily stitched together in a haphazard manner that Nash would approve of. He remains one of the most strikingly and originally inventive musicians the world has ever beheld and his instantly recognizable post-mortem sound is now more presciently post-modern than ever. Which is why . . .

NASH THE SLASH SHALL NOT DIE!

Jeffrey Morgan and
Nash The Slash,
1987

Nash The Slash
Poster
- Art Credit:
Jeffrey Morgan

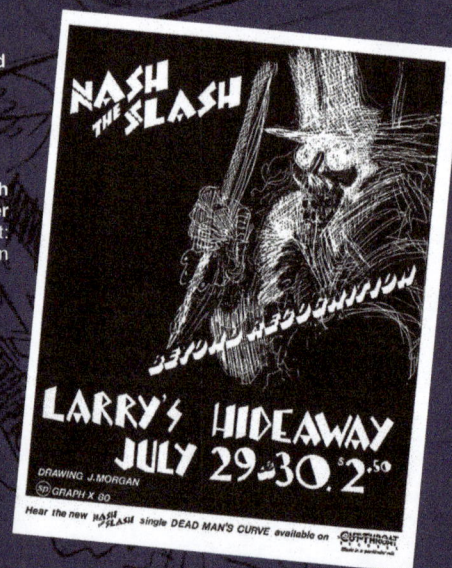

NASH THE SLASH

BEFORE RECOGNITION

LARRY'S HIDEAWAY
JULY 29-30 $2.50

DRAWING J. MORGAN
GRAPH X 80

Hear the new NASH THE SLASH single DEAD MAN'S CURVE available on CUT-THROAT

To Jeffrey Morgan I dedicate the label! Nash the Slash

"Nash The Slash, why did you leave your sticker on my forty-two dollar and fifty cent suite?" – Iggy Pop, "Eggs On Plate"

Elegantly tuxedoed like Cary Grant in George Cukor's *Holiday* and hideously bandaged like Claude Rains in James Whale's *The Invisible Man*, the revered and reviled schizo-scherzo psychotron known as Nash The Slash has been Number One in a field of one ever since he began creating his own insidious sound of music from deep within secreted studio walls located somewhere inside of an abandoned subway station miles beneath the filthy sidewalks of Toronto…

The train screamed to a slow stop inside the last station. End of the line. Stepping out onto the subway platform, I cast a nervous glance at my watch: 11:47. *Almost midnight*, I instinctively thought as I walked down the narrow ledge towards the end wall.

There right next to the blue emergency light was the door, flaked with grey paint from another era. I tried the doorknob and it gave slightly. Of course it did: *he* was waiting for me. Somewhere down…*there*.

The wrought-iron steps led down in a steep spiral. Within minutes I was more than sixty feet below the subway level. I tried to imagine how far below street level I was and shuddered slightly.

Then I heard the music—loud, brutal rock 'n' roll—and followed it some five hundred feet until I came to another door; this one small and brown, adorned with a lone silver plaque:

CUT-THROAT
J. J. Nash, prop.

I knocked twice and entered. There, before me, was a manic figure stooped over banks of tape decks and crackling Strickfaden machines, squeezing out a driving pulse of deafening 4/4 rhythm.

Suddenly, the music ceased. The figure whirled around, throwing shards of candlelight off his dark glasses. His face and hands, both covered in bandages, contorted—and there was a slight movement of gauze where the mouth should be.

"Ah, you must be from CREEM. Excuse me for not hearing you knock,"

he said, jerking his head in the direction of the pulsing machines, "but as you can see, I've been *busy*…"

Indeed. For this was no mere terminal accident victim I was in the presence of. It was Nash The Slash, The Phantom Of Rock.

"I see you're admiring my machines. *Wonderful*, aren't they?" The Slasher said, smiling at his numerous synthesizers and synthetic percussion devices. "There are two advantages to working with machines. First, they do not talk back and, second, they don't cost anything to feed—and my machines need all the diverted third rail power they can get. I need regular electricity for *other* things…"

Somewhere behind me I thought I heard the quiet hum of a plug-in freezer. I quickly put the thought out of my head.

"Perhaps your readers would be interested in hearing about my stage show," The Slasher offered. "As you know, I am—quite literally—a one man band. I create all my music using mandolin and violin; drum machines; keyboards; sequencer pedals; vocals; and numerous other devices which alter the final sound: echo, fuzz, flanger, phase…

"Visually, I perform in a totally white environment using a combination of slide and film projectors; stage props and lighting; all constructed, designed and operated by Stephen Pollard. I've worked with other designers, but only Stephen has managed to last as long as he has. Stephen used to work as an embalmer for one of the local funeral houses before I found him. His work with latex and silicone to create that fresh dead look is truly remarkable. It's *outstanding* what he can do…"

"I understand you work with two others—"

"Yes," The Slasher interrupted. "Paul Till is my personal photographer. He used to work for the Toronto *Telegram* before it folded as one of their police photographers. Toby Dammit, oddly enough, also worked for the *Tely* as a typesetter. He actually used to typeset the obituary columns. For obvious reasons, he decided to change his name when he became my lyricist. Till, on the other hand, doesn't care about using his real name; he's got nothing to lose…"

"Your shows are often extremely terrifying," I advanced. "Have you ever had any actual casualties as a result of them?"

"Yes, people have run out of the environment screaming. Others have climbed on stage waving large butcher knives, threatening to kill me. One person who was on acid jumped out of a window," laughed The Slasher. "Four

the NASHIONAL ENQUIRER
ISSUE NUMBER 1   WINTER 1980/81 $2.00

stories high. So you can understand why I cherish my privacy. Besides," The Slasher continued, waving a white gloved hand over his head, "the sound of the trains masks my music from reaching the subway patrons. Anyone who invades my territory is asking for death. *It's about having fun, but it's no joke…*"

After opening for a number of acts such as the Slits; Devo; Elvis Costello; XTC; and Ultravox, The Slasher has recently begun to invade New York with a series of concerts designed to spread the Nash Environment even further. Already he has begun to garner a fair amount of press and, during his recent New Year's Eve show at Hurrah, even Iggy Pop ushered in the '80s with The Slasher. "Only in New York City can you do a concert on New Year's Eve and realize that that same day, in 24 hours, eleven people will have been murdered," reflected The Slasher. "It's *so* inspiring…"

the NASHIONAL ENQUIRER
The Official Nash the Slash Notebook & Cut-Throat Cahier
ISSUE NUMBER 2   SPRING 1981 $2.00

I asked about his recent recording endeavors. Already with two albums to his credit, he's just released his first single on his own Cut-Throat label, Jan and Dean's vintage "Dead Man's Curve."

"Rather fitting, don't you think?" The Slasher asked, throwing his head back to laugh. "The flip side is called 'Swing Shift (Soixante-Neuf),' an original composition. My

music is now more rock 'n' roll. The music I've put on record up until now has been, essentially, film music: all instrumental, all laid back—almost classically influenced. My current live material, however, is all rock 'n' roll, and has been for a long time. I've been backlogged with so much material, but I'm catching up very quickly with my stage act on record…

"And now," The Slasher said, swinging around towards his machines, "if you'll excuse me, I have *work* to do…"

Being a man of his word, Nash The Slash proceeded to unleash upon an unsuspecting society a senses-shattering series of aural album assaults whose titles said it all: *Bedside Companion. Dreams And Nightmares. Decomposing. Children Of The Night.*

These unreasonably unrelenting records led to Nash being smuggled into Europe to work with Gary Numan and Bill Nelson, only to be abruptly expelled from the continent as "a deviant influence not only on humanity but on all life itself" after angry villagers caught a rare glimpse of his grisly ungauzed visage late one night in an iniquitous den of ill repute down on Rue Morgue Avenue.

Safely ensconced back home in his underground lair, Nash donned his stained leather apron and threw himself into his work with a renewed vengeance not seen since he was first disfigured beyond recognition—an insurrection of righteous anger that would ultimately be made manifest in the frenzied records which were to follow: the corrupt social commentary on *And You Thought You Were Normal*, the meta-industrialized urban brutality of *Thrash*, the electro-orchestral silent cinema soundtrack to *Nosferatu*, and a double-strength overdose of reimagined audio reanimations, *American BandAges* and *In-A-Gadda-Da-Nash*. Impressive, I know.

Ask any angry villager and he'll tell you there's no stopping what can't be stopped; no killing what can't be killed. So put down that pitchfork and douse that torch because they'll do you no good when Nash The Slash rises again—and he will. But don't take *my* word for it, just listen to his extensive influential life's work and see what decades of electronic sonic exotica and experimental reconstructive surgery gone horribly wrong can do for *you!*

— previously unpublished, 2021

"Giggle when you read the late Jeffrey Morgan's massive pan of Diver Down" is how CREEM introduced this feature record review when it was reprinted two years later. Van Halen didn't giggle though; indeed, the band was downright irate after reading it—hence my assumed demise. Now I'm not saying that my review was single-handedly responsible for shaming Van Halen into later recording the vastly superior 1984 but... Yeah, actually, I am.

SELLER'S MARKET

VAN HALEN
Diver Down
(Warner Bros.)

Not only is this album an insult to the average consumer who will have to pay upwards of ten dollars for it, it is an exceptionally vicious kick in the teeth to Van Halen fans everywhere; fans who—by buying their albums, attending their concerts, and wearing their merchandise—have made David Lee Roth, Alex Van Halen, Eddie Van Halen and Michael Anthony millionaires. And because I paid hard-earned money for my copy of *Diver Down*, I have a personal stake in the matter: I have been burned by Van Halen, and I don't like it.

From start to finish, this album lasts barely half an hour, which is a disgrace. In an era where the technology exists to make it feasible for someone like Todd Rundgren to release a single album of original material which lasts over an hour (*Initiation*: 67:34), there is absolutely no excuse for this kind of showing. None.

And although there *are* twelve tracks on *Diver Down*, five of them are cover versions (one lasting a mere 1:03) and three of them are guitar instrumentals (none of which is long enough to synchronize a watch by), leaving but four original songs by the band.

Of the covers, the above-noted 1:03 version of "Happy Trails" is the kind of self-indulgent filler that only reinforces my anger at Van Halen for taking advantage of their audience 'cause if you think that they would've gotten away with something like this on their first album, think again. And a note to historians who would like to point out "Mother's Lament" on *Disraeli Gears*: Don't bother, it ain't 1967 anymore.

"Dancing In The Streets," "Where Have All The Good Times Gone!" and "Pretty Woman" are so close to the original versions as to be superfluous carbon copies. Unlike their reworking of "You Really Got Me," which exuded sonic flash and style, these three remakes are merely *there*…and nothing more.

"Big Bad Bill (Is Sweet William Now)" is the kind of campy period piece that people like to crucify Freddie Mercury for, but when Freddie has written *original* material in a similar vein ("Seaside Rendezvous," "Dreamer's Ball"), the results have been at least tasteful, with none of the cheap vulgarities encountered here (to say that it's no "Take Your Whiskey Home" is an understatement).

Instrumental-wise, we're talking filler again. "Intruder" is a pale, pale imitation of the more successful "Sunday Afternoon In The Park" and the pyrotechnics which made Eddie CREEM's Guitarist Of The Year in 1981 are nowhere in sight (or sound).

As for the originals, all four songs are lame, banal exercises that don't even rock 'n' roll all that much, except for "Hang 'Em High," which is the closest thing to "classic" Van Halen on this album in terms of sheer train-out-of-control, collision-course rock 'n' roll.

Everything you loved on *Women And Children First* and *Fair Warning* are missing from *Diver Down*: the cheap asides from Roth; the glorious stereo guitar sonics; the well-crafted lyrics (yeah, well, compared to *Diver Down*, anything—including an air-raid siren—would have well-crafted lyrics); and, especially, the solid hooks which permeated almost every track.

Just when Van Halen needed to come back with a killer album to cement their status in the marketplace as the current rock 'n' roll kings, they had to go and pull a stunt like this. *Diver Down* is as bad a career move as I've ever seen—so much so that if these guys are featured in this magazine in two year's time, I'll be surprised. And don't laugh: if it happened to Aerosmith, it could happen to these bozos, too.

— CREEM, August 1982

FADE IN. JOEY: Gabba Gabba Hey! Do you know us? You'd think that us bein' America's number one rock 'n' roll band, people would. But even though we're in leather jackets and torn jeans and don't have any money, we get first class treatment wherever we go. That's 'cause we carry this.
CLOSE UP FX: Typewriter letters over credit card:

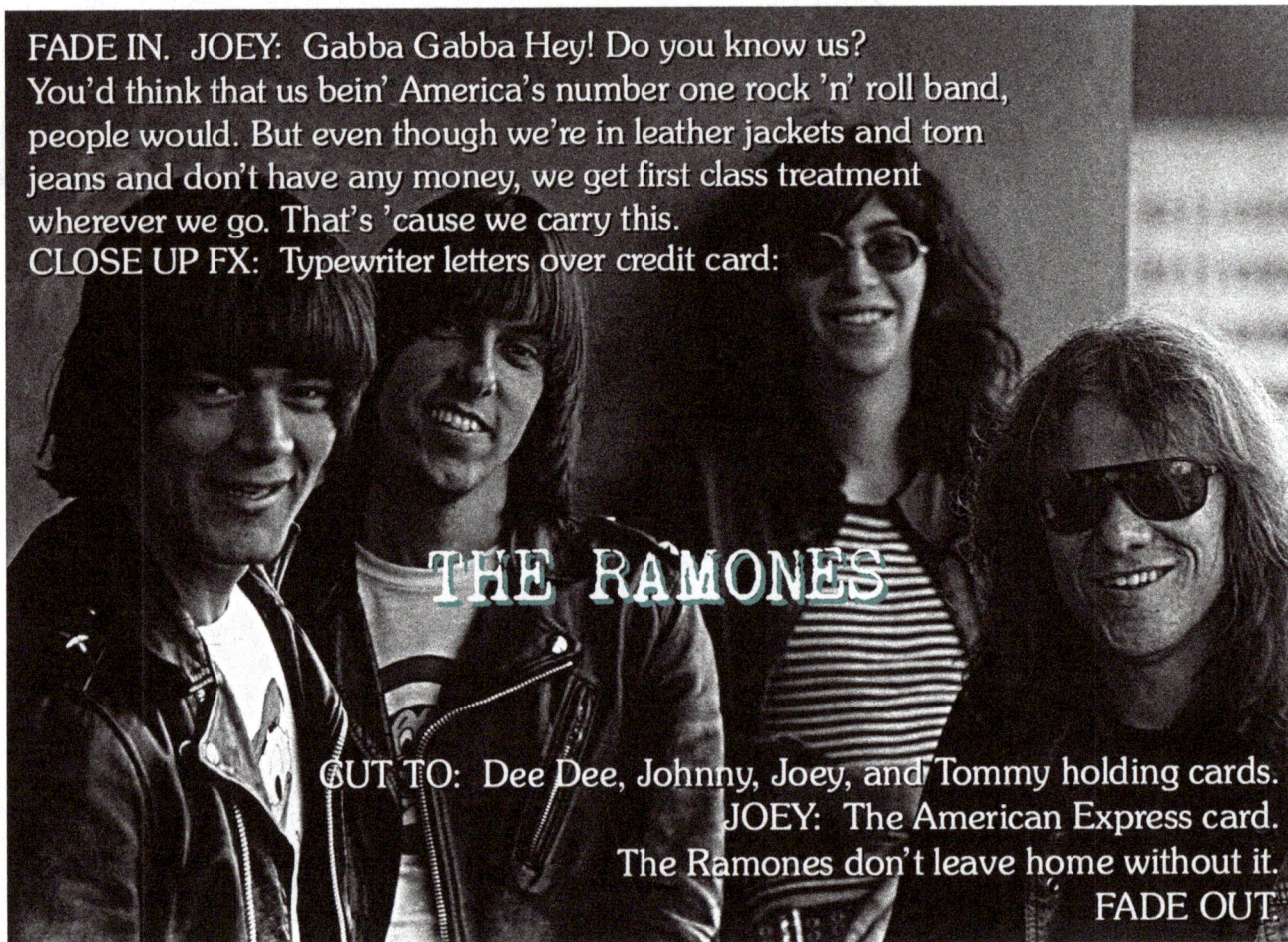

THE RAMONES

CUT TO: Dee Dee, Johnny, Joey, and Tommy holding cards.
JOEY: The American Express card.
The Ramones don't leave home without it.
FADE OUT

Photograph © Ralph Alfonso

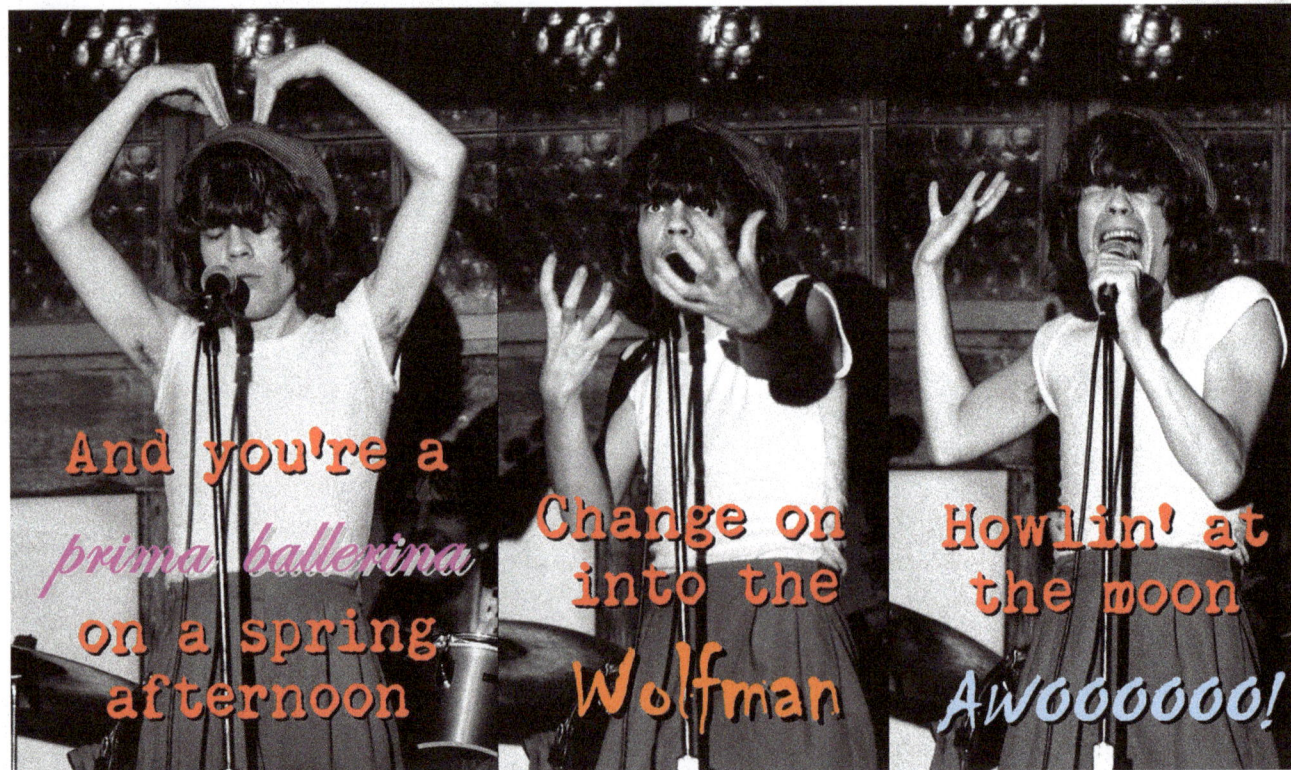

And you're a *prima ballerina* on a spring afternoon

Change on into the Wolfman

Howlin' at the moon Awoooooo!

The following biography was originally written for an authorized Dr. John box set. However, just as the accompanying book containing Robert Matheu's photographs and Jeffrey Morgan's words was about to go to press, the record company reneged when it received a mysterious summons which strongly suggested, in no uncertain terms, that our work not be published. Luckily, us Script Doctors don't threaten so easily.

THE UNFAMILIAR REALITY AND AUTHORIZED MYTHOLOGY OF

DR. JOHN, THE NIGHT TRIPPER

"***Look***, I can't *take* any more of this from you, LaRue! Now for the *last time* I'm *tellin'* ya: I ain't wearin' *no* grass skoits! And I *ain't* singin' no 'Tiny Bubbles' *neither!*" — Dr. John to Johnny LaRue in *Polynesiantown*, 1981

☆☆☆

"So you want to know about the Doctor." Mamzoux leans forward and snares me with a hypnotic stare before abruptly breaking the connection to look down and roll another cigarette. As her long fingernails herd the shreds of tobacco into place, they scrape against the scarred wooden table top and sound like driver ants hollowing out a snakeskin.

"That's why everybody tries to locate me," she continues in a husky monotone before deftly licking the fixings into place. "They all try and they all go away empty handed."

Igniting a match against the table, Mamzoux torches the paper and deeply inhales the acrid smoke before locking eyes with me again. "Why should *you* be any different?" she asks. "Because you've heard some *records?* Some *stories?* What do *you* know about the Doctor, anyway?"

I shifted uneasily in my chair. It was a good question. Obviously I didn't know nearly enough or else I would never have dared to wade deep-knee through a series of brackish backwater swamps

in search of the wizened woman they called with fearful respect the Last of the Elder Hoodoo Queens.

After several months of frustrating failed attempts and a series of perilous close calls which involved at least one protracted period of recuperation, I finally found the arcane entrance to where she plied her craft in a heretofore hidden tributary on the Bayouk Choupic that suddenly appeared where previously there was no opening to be seen.

Inside, her candlelit quarters were exactly as I'd seen them in my recurring dreams but what I wasn't prepared for was that she had been expecting me; indeed, that she was patiently waiting for me all this time and knew precisely why I had come.

"Of course," she says. "I've read your authorized biographies. Melodramatic, but they speak the truth. Which is why I brought you here and allowed you to find me. You went to the well to wash your toe so *I'll* tell you what you know and what you *don't* know, beginning with the *original* Doctor John.

"Once upon a time there was a certain Prince John de Legendre who was known in New Orleans during the middle 1880s as 'The Doctor.' When he wasn't living up to his name by creating cure-all potions, he was foretelling the future by presiding over a series of séances and ceremonies during which he served as a living link between the past and the present and the future. What *isn't* known

is that, just before he died, Doctor John vowed that he would rend this final veil and return when the time was right and his enduring expertise was most needed.

"Naturally, there will always be those who prefer to shroud themselves in a deceiving skein of false security and accept as true a *safer* story with a more *benign* beginning: namely, that 'Dr. John' is merely a put-on persona and that 'Mac Rebennack' is the wearer when, in fact, it is the other way around.

☆☆☆

"*Dr. John is Doctor John incarnate as Mac Rebennack.*"

☆☆☆

When I rise in surprise at this mind-reeling revelation which inverts and subverts everything I had been led to believe about one of the world's most mystifying musicians, Mamzoux dismisses my disbelief and instructs me to regain my seat with a curt gesture. As I do, I briefly glimpse the imposing shadow of someone standing close behind the semi-translucent wall of curtains which brush against the back of Mamzoux's wicker throne. Then, as if concurrent with an abrupt wind-caught flickering of the table's candle, the dusky outline ebbs away.

"For a century," Mamzoux elaborates, "the undying essence of Doctor John lay dormant, patiently waiting for the right socio-celestial alignment to present itself. That moment came with the

November 1940 birth of Mac Rebennack in New Orleans. Less than a year later, these psyche-societal emanations were made manifest when the nine-month-old Louisiana child's visage appeared on the cover of Ivory Soap boxes all across America.

"So began his subliminal seduction of a world which wouldn't behold him in the full glory of his *bona fide* form for another three decades. But first there were many lessons to be learned. For contemporaneous music would be the method by which his medicinal message would be spread. These songs would be the enveloping cure-alls which would literally be heard around the world.

"His education was initiated by the rare roots platters spun on the family Victrola,

followed soon thereafter by the purchase of a six-string signifier upon which he learned to duplicate those records with a precision some whispered was preternatural. It wasn't long before he stole out of the house at the stroke of midnight, compelled to attend nocturnal concerts held on the outskirts of town by the legendary likes of Longhair and Papoose.

"Over time, this instrumental dexterity saw his life accelerate into a dizzying whirlwind of bands and studios and clubs during which the ancient art of mixing remedies was transmogrified into a more modern means whereby he could arrange a myriad of notes into melodies which, when heard, could have either an innocent or an ominous effect, depending on their intent. Only then was

he ready to experience the next life-altering step."

☆☆☆

Mamzoux drops the dwindled cigarette into a rusty can and immediately begins assembling a new one. As she does, I try to ignore the irregular skittering sounds and concentrate instead on what she'd said. Although sparse, the skeletal facts she related about Mac's early life were but a litany of well-known truisms that could be read about in greater detail in any of the biographies or purported collected recollections which had been published over the years.

What *wasn't* in any of them, however, was the heretofore unknown revelatory inference that the Dr. John of the present was in reality the Doctor John of the past. As for the life-altering next step in his life, the only thing I could think of that could possible fit that description would be Mac's—

"*Accident?*" Mamzoux draws deeply on her fresh cigarette and slowly exhales. "There are no accidents," she resumes in a matter of fact tone of voice. "All is a predestined path leading to destiny. When a gun is discharged during a motel fight and the bullet hits a guitarist in his left index finger ending his career on his chosen instrument, that is no accident. It is a divergence in the same eternity; one which led to his eventual mastery of the keyboard and the final apogee of his ability as a songwriter and arranger. After which, it was only a matter of waiting until society had evolved enough to hear what he had to say when he said it under the more apposite designation of Dr. John Creaux."

When I comment that "what he had to say" was said on *Gris-Gris* and *Babylon* and *Remedies* and *The Sun, Moon & Herbs* and *Dr. John's Gumbo*, Mamzoux nods knowingly.

"They were just the beginning, for each of the Doctor's albums is a sonic sachet full of potent audio potions." Mamzoux leans forward and the wicker creaks with the movement. "*No one who hears them is ever the same again.*"

I then mention that, according to conventional wisdom, those albums were well received because they fitted into what was musically in vogue at the time.

"Conventional, perhaps. Wisdom, perhaps not." Mamzoux leans back and taps a roll of ash into the can. "White men dressed as women singing about *black juju* and black women dressed as men singing about *taboo voodoo* were a part of the popular culture whereby an open portal was created through which the Doctor could now reach into the lives of untold millions in a way he never could before.

Dr John Photo © Robert Matheu

Dr John Photo © Robert Matheu

"Then, once ingrained, he could afford to transmute the time-honored trappings of his physical schema and present a more mainstream façade to further extend his influence. Thus, the gradual visual shift which accompanied his hit singles 'Right Place Wrong Time' and 'Such A Night' on *In The Right Place*. From that point on, he could assertively advance in any direction he desired, free from all aesthetic constraints."

Which explains why—

"Yes," Mamzoux says solemnly. "Once Doctor John garnered awareness as Dr. John, it was Mac Rebennack's turn to convert that attention into affection by the adept application of a dual duplicity which went unnoticed despite the occasional allusion provided by overt album titles like *Dr. John Sings Mac Rebennack*.

"Hence, he sang standards ranging from Cole Porter to Duke Ellington; smiled in the spotlight during *The Last Waltz*; and, in his most disarmingly charming recital, wore an Hawaiian-styled shirt while literally performing drop dead comedy in the SCTV production of *Polynesiantown*. As decade begat decade and century begat century, every note he played, be it reverent or ribald, conveyed an age-old spellbinding subtext.

"And now, after all that time, who is in the Rock Hall? Whose name is honored and whose face is on display? Mac Rebennack?" Mamzoux laughs. "*The Doctor*."

She extends a gnarled hand. "Give me the track listing."

I stammer out something but Mamzoux cuts me off with another curt gesture. "If you are going to relay the Doctor's music publicly by the use of three vinyl records, you must be certain of the consequences. Vinyl amplifies psychic emanations, resulting in powerful resonations."

Pulling a crumpled piece of paper from my pocket, I place it in her hand and Mamzoux withdraws it for inspection. "Are you *sure* you want to use these?" she asks. "Because playing these songs in this particular order will…"

Without waiting for a reply, Mamzoux shrugs and lifts her arm to hold the paper over her shoulder. I look up and watch as a ringed hand silently emerges from an opening in the curtains and takes the paper before withdrawing back through the cloth.

☆☆☆

Then I hear the sound of urgent scribbling and a raspy voice chuckling: "*Ti boul ti nan diven an*."

Suddenly Mamzoux claps her hands together. "You must be tired after your long journey." Reaching under the table, she pulls out an old wine skin and a chalice.

"Here," she says, pouring out a small amount of viscous liquid. "Gumption for your return trip."

Mamzoux slides the chalice across the table and her eyes lock onto mine. "Drink."

As I do, the scribbling sound stops and the hand reappears through the curtains, holding a piece of parchment.

Reaching back, Mamzoux takes the parchment from the already vanishing hand and glances at it. Then, for the first time during my stay, she smiles briefly before holding it to me. "*These* songs. In *this* sequence."

"These songs. In this sequence," I repeat dully as I take possession of it.

"*Touch the surface, touch the soul*," Mamzoux chants. "*Transmit the writ, message takes hold*."

And the last thing I see is a turbaned figure emerging through the curtains in a regalia of robes adorned with feathers and bones.

And the last thing I hear is a raspy voice intoning: "*I'm the only one that'll tell ya the truth and I tell ya I'm the one who knows*."

— previously unpublished, 2014

SUZI QUATRO

GEORGE HARRISON & BILLY PRESTON

EDDIE JOBSON

JEFFERSON STARSHIP

"*I was awed. You controlled that interview with such grace. I have never witnessed anyone getting such admissions out of him. It was perfect. Beyond great.*" — Jaan Uhelszki

THE DEFINITIVE TED NUGENT INTERVIEW

TED NUGENT: Did you see the show, Jeffrey?

JEFFREY MORGAN: It sounded good. You didn't disappoint.

NUGENT: All right, all right! You got questions, I got answers. I'm ready to rock! Yeah, I'm game for basically anything, Jeffrey. I'm saying let 'er rip. Actually, you might want to just start flinging questions at me now 'cause, *God am I full of ideas*.

☆☆☆

MORGAN: Got a little history, too, I wanna talk about.

NUGENT: I'll be playing my 24th year at Cobo Hall next week.

MORGAN: I thought it'd be 23. 1965, wasn't it?

NUGENT: 1963 with The Supremes. I had a silver sharkskin suit on with black Beatle boots I got from Denim Brothers— a nigger shop. A nigger shop. Beatle boots with the black elastic. And I played a white Fender Duo-Sonic through a white Bandmaster. We opened up with "Shake Your Tail Feather" to "Little By Little" off the first Rolling Stones album.

MORGAN: You actually remember being on stage.

NUGENT: Oh yeah. Yeah, because you know why? The Supremes' entire Motown orchestra was beside us. They *had* to stay in their seats while we were playing. They had a little area on the stage about like *this* [*gestures*] with all these big niggers over there with their horns. Fuckin' great. And they're diggin'. I come flingin' across the stage, rip my fucking knees outta my suit. I was only thirteen. I was a *wild* thirteen. Now I'm all matured. And at Cobo Hall at the end of the month, we're gonna play "Journey To The Center Of Your Mind."

MORGAN: When they play that on the radio today, it's still heaver than—

NUGENT: A lotta stuff. *Especially nowadays!* It makes everything else sound like a Kinney shoe commercial.

MORGAN: You got any people asking you to give *your* songs out for commercials? Anybody wanna license "Wang Dang"?

NUGENT: Dr. Pepper wanted to use "Just What The Doctor Ordered."

MORGAN: When you talked to CREEM's Billy Altman—

NUGENT: Billy!

MORGAN: …about ten years ago—

NUGENT: [*laughs*] Yeah, a little while ago.

MORGAN: …you said you wanted him on *your* side. But your side seems to be in the middle now.

NUGENT: I like to look at it that the *world* is Ted's turf.

MORGAN: Well, tonight wasn't a bad show. But the *best* show I've ever seen you give was the first time I saw you. You were about 23, 24.

NUGENT: Just a boy.

MORGAN: Fifteen years ago. You came in—

NUGENT: Was it the opening for Grand Funk?

MORGAN: No, better than that. You played a comic book convention here in the city.

NUGENT: *Get the fuck outta here!*

MORGAN: I was there and there must've been 30, 40 people . . .

NUGENT: Amboy Dukes?

MORGAN: Yeah.

NUGENT: *Still Amboy Dukes?* Son of a bitch. *A comic book convention?*

MORGAN: Sunday, January the 28th, 1973. This is four or five months before you recorded—

NUGENT: That would be a three piece. Rob Grange, Billy Grange, and Vic Mastriani.

MORGAN: This is before you started recording *Call Of The Wild*.

NUGENT: That's right.

MORGAN: So the material you were

doing was "Rattle My Snake," "Papa's Will"…

NUGENT: *Rattle my fuckin' snake*. Cool. "Papa's Will," *what a fuckin' masterpiece*.

MORGAN: You do any of those anymore?

NUGENT: No. These cocksucking people today would go: "Will you write good…" They don't *listen* today. You know, I got into this…*business*… Well, first of all, I didn't know it was a *business*. In fact, it *wasn't* a business when I got into it. But I got into this maneuver because it was the ultimate expression of *independence*. You turn that fucking amp on and *do what you fucking please*, Captain. You know what I mean? And that attitude is *still* the only attitude. I get all kinds of recommendations: "Well, you should do this song." "Thank you for your recommendation but I will do what I like."

I'm opening up for KISS 'cause they're going to draw a slamming audience who want to just power out. So I'll focus on some power tunes. But you can't call "Hey Baby" a power tune. "Hey Baby" is a be-bopper, man.

MORGAN: Well, I'm glad to see that you've got Mister St. Holmes on the stage again doing it.

NUGENT: Damn right.

DEREK ST. HOLMES: Well, thank you very much.

MORGAN: Now if I can get serious for a moment…

NUGENT: Go for it, man.

MORGAN: About your album titles—

NUGENT: They *are* grand, aren't they?

MORGAN: Now hold on a second here, the jury's still out on that. You started out with album titles like *Survival Of The Fittest*, then *Tooth, Fang & Claw*...

NUGENT: Another environmentally sound—

MORGAN: …and *Call Of The Wild*, which contained social commentary in songs like "Cannonball" and "Pony Express." Now by this point you've crafted an image as an outspoken advocate with a little bit of nobility; an image that carries over into the first solo album.

NUGENT: Yeah.

MORGAN: And then all of a sudden we get *Scream Dream*, "Wango Tango," *Weekend Warriors*—

NUGENT: Overt fun and games.

MORGAN: …to the point where you've gone from being a noble savage to a cartoon character.

NUGENT: [*quietly*] You think so?

MORGAN: *Yeah!* There's *miles* of distance between the nobility of *Survival Of The Fittest* to the cover of *Intensities In Ten Cities*. The man on the cover of *Intensities In Ten Cities* should've been hawking cartoons on Saturday morning.

NUGENT: Okay.

MORGAN: I understand the satire there, and I'm not begrudging you that. But I'm just saying: looking at that, were you—

NUGENT: *Totally* unconscious. Totally unconscious.

MORGAN: So you just took the ball and ran with it.

NUGENT: I…I wasn't even aware that I *had* the ball, I was just *running*.

MORGAN: But didn't you ever wake up and look back and realize that you were looking a little foolish?

NUGENT: Never thought of it until you

> ## I was not a hippie.
> ### - Ted Nugent

just brought it up now.

MORGAN: Those early albums were predatory. They had teeth. They had impact. And then the rest of them got soft and hokey and vaudeville.

NUGENT: Well, okay. I can acknowledge that, and also tell you *why*.

MORGAN: All right, go.

NUGENT: I was born. Somewhere down the road I'm gonna die. *No one*, since the dawn of man, is gonna have more fun than I am between those two points. *No one*. And in pursuit of this right of Americans to pursue happiness, I have pursued it, tackled it, devoured it, puked it, and snorted its remains numerous times. And I hope you got that on tape because I want a copy of it.

MORGAN: [*silence*] *You* know what I

mean.

NUGENT: Yeah, I *do* know what you're getting at. You know what my biggest problem in life is? I'm my own worst enemy because I am too intense for my own good.

MORGAN: You can't say no to yourself?

NUGENT: Oh, I can say no like a champ. But I don't *want* to when it comes time for rock 'n' roll. And I don't remember ever saying that. So what I *do* is, I *don't* think about the motivation of the song. Obviously over the…when I started—

MORGAN: In other words, you were losing a little respect towards Columbia.

NUGENT: Well I *must've* because it sure didn't translate into sales, did it? But I didn't really know that respect *went* with sales. Because I could say a few things about *that*. And you're right: I'm *not* motivated in my music to write "Great White Buffalo" and *Tooth, Fang & Claw* and "Call Of The Wild" and "Pony Express" anymore because—

MORGAN: It's a losing battle?

NUGENT: No, no, no. Not at all, not at all. My hunting is my hunting. My music is *one…big..hard on*. Literally. Sex plays an *outlandish* role in the whole Ted Nugent rock 'n' roll thing.

MORGAN: Where's the tie-in, though? What's the excuse for not writing songs like "Pony Express" anymore?

Ted Nugent Photo © Robert Matheu

NUGENT: Because I am *overwhelmed* and *consumed* by beautiful firm women. It's so fucking incredible that it motivates every song. Listen to the fuckin' lyrics!

MORGAN: In other words, you're too *busy* these days to notice that the mail's late.

NUGENT: Absolutely.

MORGAN: You're obsessed!

NUGENT: I'm obsessed.

MORGAN: Are you still a hard case on drugs?

NUGENT: *Real* hard. I have never done a drug in my life. I have never smoked a joint in my life. I took two tokes off a joint with the MC5 one night and almost *gagged* and thought it was *stupid*. And that's *it*. I took two tokes off a joint once. I snorted one line of cocaine. And one line of crystal methedrine before my draft physical—*but God, that was worth it because I wanted to see the look on the Sergeant's face*. That's *it* for drugs.

I went through a basic period in my life of saying [*softly*] "No, no thanks" to a period of [*yelling*] "NO! GET HIM THE FUCK OUTTA HERE!" to when people would offer it to me I would just go *fuckin' nuts*. People would offer me drugs and it was just like they were holding a *razor* to my fuckin' arm. And I'd go *wild* because I considered it an *affront*.

Because every time we were *late*, every time an *amp* didn't work, every time a *car* wasn't serviced, every time there was a *fuck up*, it was because *someone was stoned*. PERIOD! And it was a fuckin' *thorn in my side* and I kicked fuckin' ass. It was the only way I was able to clean house. And the only way I could impress people to keep the fuck… I've had guys come at me and go: [*in a slurred voice*] "Uh, wow, Ted. How y'doin' man? Right on. Uh, where's your Strat? Your *Strat*, man. C'mon, you *always* played a Strat! The time we did the *cocaine* together you were playin' the St—" [*screaming*] "GET THE FUCK *OUTTA* HERE! *I NEVER PLAYED A STRAT IN MY LIFE!*"

MORGAN: So you just say no.

NUGENT: I say fuckin' no, loud and fuckin' clear with a large caliber fuckin' weapon. How many of them are even *alive* today? How many are in *jail* today? How many *talk* like the Special Olympics of conversation today? How many *drool* when they look at you? *Fuck them*. I *laugh* at them. I laugh in their *face*. When they fall and die, *I laugh*. I go, "Let's fuckin' celebrate. I'm buying Vernors for everybody, the asshole died on drugs." [*laughs*] *Fuck 'em all*.

I've never had a drug in my body. I've never had a cigarette in my mouth. No big deal, it's not like a big ceremony for me. It's not like [*in a lofty voice*] "*Yes, and I'm salvation itself…*" Big rat's ass, it's my

own personal little thing. And I'm *better* because of it. I'm *faster* than most people. I'm having *way* more fun than most people. *And I'm alive*. And I don't choke on my own vomit. [*laughs*]

MORGAN: Then what were you doing playing a drug dealer on *Miami Vice*?

NUGENT: *Acting*. I'd've played a *fag* if it was a good part—and God knows I ain't endorsin' *that* shit.

☆☆☆

MORGAN: You mentioned the MC5…

NUGENT: I used to go to the 5 all the time and try to be friends with them, but they were so *stoned* it was like talkin' to a fuckin' *log*.

MORGAN: Were you ever approached by John Sinclair to support the White Panthers' Rainbow People's Party?

NUGENT: Many people, many times. I was fascinated by it because I was a major fan of the 5, and I was a major fan of what I thought was a camaraderie there. *Not a commune*. Not a bunch of dope smokin' pieces of ass fuck. I said, "I want to know about this people's party." And, you know, he's gagging on a joint, and I realized there wasn't a whole lot to talk about. You know, he *smelled* like a fuckin' hippie, he *looked* like a fuckin' hippie, he smoked all kinds of fuckin' dope and I said: "No, John. Fuck you."

And I was *outcast*. Those people made fun of me at *every* chance. And I made sure I gave them all the opportunities in the world because I'd come to their parties and *pretend* I was stoned. And I'd end up taking my pants down to my knees and *sitting* in the brown rice. They want to see somebody stoned, *I'll* show 'em somebody fuckin' stoned.

MORGAN: Would your music have been different in some way if you'd grown up in Chicago or New York as opposed to Detroit?

NUGENT: I don't think it would've mattered. I have a funny feeling that what you see right here, this is exactly what it would be.

MORGAN: I don't know, I can't see you being like *this* if you'd grown up here in Toronto.

NUGENT: I guarantee you I would have been. First of all, I'd have gotten *out* of here so I could get a Smith & Wesson.

MORGAN: Did you see *Death Wish*?

NUGENT: Yeah, I *loved* that. *Oh*, loved it. But I was too close to it. I didn't believe in it as a movie, I believed in it as a *social reality*.

MORGAN: Well, it's "Stormtroopin'."

NUGENT: That's "Stormtroopin' " in a fuckin' *nutshell*. Independence. Standing up for something. Did you see on the last album I thanked Bernie Goetz?

MORGAN: How did you feel about him getting six months?

NUGENT: I think it *sucks*. I think it sucks. And anybody who thinks that he was wrong is a complete *asshole* and a victim of the Special Olympics of modern society. The typical human being is in a Special Olympics mode of life. I think it's deplorable. I think it's a typical case of the world turned upside down, that we live in. That justice *does not* exist and that what's right and wrong is upside fuckin' down.

He shoulda shot those four cocksuckers *dead*. And he shoulda been given an award. *Period*. Get them cocksuckers outta the gene pool. Get 'em fuckin' *outta here*. The society we live in now has pampered and promoted *predatorship* in man's world.

The left are obviously mentally retarded. People actually came out and *criticized* him for blowing these dirty cocksuckers away and tried to put them on a pedestal, saying they were victims. When they were vicious, evil, preying *bastards* that have *mutilated*, hurt and *ruined* lives. And they tried to say that these poor little savages were victimized by Bernie, *defending* him-fuckin'-self. Did I *miss* something?

The only guy that didn't continue *preying* on society was the one who was *paralyzed*! And if he wasn't *paralyzed*, he'd been right out there fucking with people. You *know* that! Who could *possibly* defend these cocksuckers? I mean, we are alive, we are working, and

> ## "Detroit isn't more violent, we just shoot a little better.
> ### - Ted Nugent"

we are earning our way and we are getting from point A to point B and these motherfuckers step in our way and they take our lives and they mutilate us and they rape our people and they rape our children and they ruin our lives and mutilate our psyches . . .

What are we sup... May I suggest we *eliminate* them? May I suggest that when we encounter them we are *not* unarmed like the fucking *feeble* Canadians who aren't even allowed to be *trusted* with fucking guns but, rather, we have a gun and we say: "Oh, my wallet? *You* want my wallet? I've worked my fucking *ass* off to earn this cash and *you* want it on a *whim*? KA-FUCKIN'-POW, motherfucker!" One more *outta* the fuckin' system. Get him the fuck... *Mulch* him, put him in a blender, pour him on my garden and enhance my veggies. Get him the *fuck* outta the gene pool. *Do not* let him fuckin' multiply.

Right now the asswipes are being *flowed* outta the prisons, they're *fuckin'*, they're having babies, and *their* babies are *fucked*. Half the niggers in the world don't e—*I don't even care how you edit this*—half the fucking niggers in the world don't even *know* who their fucking parents are. They go out and they learn a life of fuckin' deceit, deception, robbery and fuckin' *viciousness* and they're given: "Well, he only killed three people, we'll put him on parole." *Fuck* the parole officer, *fuck* the guy who *did* it, fuck everybody who's got any of his fuckin' *bloodline*. Cocksuckers are *preying* on us.

MORGAN: What about the judges?

NUGENT: Fuck the judges, man. Blow *them* cocksuckers *right* away. I *really* have a horrible pent-up... But man, what, 40 cents out of every dollar I make goes to *support* these pieces of shit? And a system that *will not* protect you and *me*...

And we're gonna get a speeding ticket, we're gonna get busted at the border for not having our zipper all the way up but, meanwhile, these cocksuckers are *pillaging* the earth. They're out on the fucking *street* 'cause there's not enough *bed* with the proper amount of *cushion* on it in the *jail* for them!

Did I *miss* something? Is this upside-fucking-down? *The left can suck my dead*

dog's dick. That's what the *left* can do. "Angry Young Man"? [*hits Morgan in the shoulder*] I'm *still* making social comments. That song's a social commentary.

MORGAN: Let me read you a quote from James Brown's biography.

NUGENT: Oh, yeah? *James*! One of my... When I use the term "nigger," I mean...*you* know what I'm saying. James is my hero of all time. Number one entertainer, number one *hero* of my life.

MORGAN: You're the James Brown of rock 'n' roll.

NUGENT: You *think* so?

MORGAN: Hardest working man in rock 'n' roll.

NUGENT: Damned *right* I am. Nobody even comes *close*.

MORGAN: Here's a quote from James: "I'm for peace, always have been. But I will protect myself. I will take a life if I saw mine was going to be threatened." That's James in 1986. Here's Ted in 1976: "I believe in justice. I believe that if someone attempts to take my life and fails, I have the right to take his."

NUGENT: Absolutely.

MORGAN: You know what comes after this?

NUGENT: No.

MORGAN: The line where you go: "And I did. I killed two guys." That was in CREEM.

NUGENT: [*quietly*] Yeah, it was in CREEM.

MORGAN: Now, was that a fact?

NUGENT: Yeah, well...

MORGAN: On or off?

NUGENT: It's already been written and I'd rather have it off.

MORGAN: Off the record?

NUGENT: Yeah.

☆☆☆

[CONVERSATION CONTINUES OFF THE RECORD THEN RESUMES]

☆☆☆

NUGENT: Anyhow... Um... Yeah... I haven't even *talked* about that story for a long time. But...*fuck 'em*. They— I mean, it was just a... I mean, how many robberies have happened like that when they shoot and *then* they take your shit? He just thought I... Y'see, back then they thought we were all hippies. Meanwhile, these *asswipe* fucking hipples, the MC5 and all *those* other pieces of dog shit, had their guns and revolution. They were *fake fuckin' guns* and they were out smokin' dope and eating brown rice. I was driving my limo, picking up chicks, and getting my *dick* wet. *Fuck* these fuckin' hippies. I was *not* a hippie.

But these fuckin' niggers *thought* I was a hippie and they went: "Let's take the hippie's money." [*laughs and claps hands*] "Good *morning*, nigger. The long-haired fuckin' *battle dog* is on call." And you both fuckin' *died*. And the *one* died in the *worst* fear—worse than any plane crash victim has ever been scared to death. He was *dead* before he even crawled *away* from me.

If you think I got intense when I used to do "Papa's Will" or I get intense when I do screams and shit on stage, *that's snoozing*. I'm fuckin' *asleep*. I'm *comatose* when I'm doing *that* shit

compared to that moment. And a couple of other moments in my life when assholes brought out...*the dog*. And, *God*, do I feel *great* afterwards 'cause it's about time they came to an abrupt [*claps hands*] fuckin' *halt* in their viciousness. There was a couple of other times...just been *outrageous*...which inspired a lot of what makes me tick.

MORGAN: Yeah, but for a couple of days afterwards...

NUGENT: Huh?

MORGAN: Looking around the corner were you a little shaky?

NUGENT: I was...I was...absolutely *beside* myself for months after that. I

wasn't paranoid but...I don't think I *smiled* for ten days.

MORGAN: Were you afraid that someone was going to find out?

NUGENT: I wasn't afraid *at all*. I was *hopin'* they'd take me through the *fuckin'* system and I'd say: "Yeah!" and I'd've got up and I'd have my light man put *lights* on me and go: "*Yeah*, I fuckin' shot 'em, huh? What is *that* for fucking accuracy, motherfucker?" I *wish* some shit like that'd come out because, when it gets right down to it, society *needs* to be exposed to more *justice*.

And there have been many cases since where... There was a mother in Chicago in 19... I dunno, it was '83 or '84. This nine-year-old little girl had been raped by this guy twice before and *she* knew he did it, and *they* knew he did it, but they couldn't get the little girl...she was so panic-stricken they couldn't get her to testify. So the mother said, "Can *I* make a statement, your Honor, on the record?" And he goes, "Well, it's out of order but, yeah, go ahead." And she walked over, she walked up to this guy who was handcuffed, she took out a .45 and *emptied* the fucking clip on him. Killed him dead. They pressed charges but it was thrown out of court.

I mean, *fuck* these people, man. It's ugly, and it's not right, *but it's necessary*.

Bernie Goetz shouldn't've just plugged them with a .38, he shoulda fuckin' hosed 'em down with some good ammo and *killed* those cocksuckers. We don't *need* those people, man. They *cost* us, and I'm not talking about cash now, I'm talking *lives* and *emotion* and *pain* and *fear*. Society in general is pretty fucking vicious. And, basically, the vicious people are getting more vicious and the wimps are getting more wimpy.

MORGAN: What's the worst city for that?

NUGENT: Oh, *take your pick*, any hour of the day. I mean, New York's got plenty of action. Detroit isn't more violent than anybody else, we just shoot a little better. You wanna see crime, go to places where *wimps rule*. New York City, you're *not* allowed to own a gun so there's crime everywhere. Cody, Wyoming? *There's no fucking crime in Cody, Wyoming.*

> " *The left are obviously mentally retarded.*
>
> - Ted Nugent "

Everybody's got a fucking *Ruger* in their fucking pocket.

I think that anybody who's *robbed* and *gives in* or is *raped* and *gives in* or says: [*in a timid voice*] "Oooh, I don't want to carry a gun, they *scare* me…" Then I hope your *ass* bleeds when you get raped. I hope he's got a dick *that big around*. Because what you're *doing* is, when you're *taking* it, you're saying: [*in a strained voice*] "Yeah, well…oh…yeah… we're *accepting* this" [*grunts*] "We're accepting it. You know, *I'm* not resisting." Criminals have the *red carpet* laid out for them. [*in a timid voice*] "*Take* us, no resistance here." Meanwhile, they oughtta blow him a-fuckin'-way, piece by piece. *Man*, do I believe in that. *Boy*, do I believe in that.

Look at what happened to Bernie. Crime didn't go *down* that week, *it vanished*. There was *not one*… Those kind of confrontations, what'd they figure there were? One every four hours or something on that one subway until Bernie *shot* the four pieces of shit? And then it didn't go down…*it vanished for two fucking weeks*. Until they brought charges against the son of a bitch and all of a sudden the criminals went: "Yeah, they're protecting us, let's start over again." Did I *miss* something here?

Shoot the cocksuckers, shoot 'em *regularly*, and they will find a *new* line of fuckin' work, I guaran-fuckin'-tee it. I'm not talkin' about any potential scenario, I'm talkin' about what is black and fuckin' white. *Shoot* the cocksucker and he *ain't* gonna rob you again. *Period*. If he *robs* you, put him in jail for a *long* fuckin' time and *beat* him pretty often. And I guarantee you when he gets out—if we decide to *let* him out—he *ain't* gonna try that shit again.

Canada is a great case in point. *I* don't bring my gun to Canada. I stop at the State Police Post on the U.S. side and I give 'em my .44. "Would you guys hold this for me while I go to this Communist country?" [*laughter*] Yet they allow you to bring *shotguns* in but *not a hand gun*. So I leave my .44 at the border and I bring in a 12 gauge shotgun, *no problem*. Let's get after the bad guys. Please focus on the bad guys.

MORGAN: Too many people are getting too many rights in this world?

NUGENT: Absolutely. Absolutely. Too many of the *wrong* people are getting the *wrong* rights.

MORGAN: And all the wrong ones are walking?

NUGENT: You bet. I mean, how *dare* they send these *vicious, heinous criminals* back on the streets because they're *out of beds*? Or because they forgot to read him his rights as they pulled his knife out of the little girl's chest? There's a general

> ## "
> ## *May I suggest we eliminate them?*
> ## - Ted Nugent
> ## "

right and wrong premise that we should all function under, and that is gone in the wind.

MORGAN: Do you ever wonder what the hell is going on?

NUGENT: Oh, I'm *constantly* wondering what the hell's going on because this is not the world that I would have.

MORGAN: It's not the world you started out in, that's for sure.

NUGENT: No, it isn't. Not at all. It's mostly *crime* and *evil* oriented.

MORGAN: A lot of people don't seem to have a good grip on separating reality from fantasy.

NUGENT: I'll buy *that* shit. I'm sure of that. I bought some stuff from a drug store where she didn't know how to work the cash register. Ineptness is promoted in the world, there's no doubt about it. "You don't have to be qualified, *here's your job*." [*laughs*] I hate to be so *fucking critical* of people but… I'll tell you where our society is at… [*sighs*] God help us all.

There are packs of wild dogs around the country that spread disease. We had a bus stop situation here last year near my home in Michigan where a little girl, a nine year old girl, was *mauled* by a pack of dogs. And they were all Fido and Fifi, they all had collars on, they all had Alpo breath. And they attacked the kids at the bus stop and mauled this little girl.

In pack form, they revert to their wild instincts. They suck down the Ken-L Ration at night and when the people go to bed they go roam out and they kill deer and they kill game and they attack kids at bus stops.

Well, the animal control officer came back, they found the pack of dogs, but he said: "I couldn't get close enough for the net." So meanwhile, *at the cost of mauled children*, you don't *shoot* 'em for public image? *Shoot* the fuckin' dogs, *I'll* shoot 'em!

MORGAN: Sounds like the pit bull problem.

NUGENT: Yeah! Fuck, *shoot* the cocksuckers! *Why does everybody think everything is so*…

MORGAN: Sacred?

NUGENT: [*laughs*] Give me a fuckin'

break! Fido's sacred as long as he sits in your lap and wags his tail. When he starts molesting kids and attacking them at bus stops, *blow him a-fuckin'-way*.

MORGAN: Do you meet a lot of people who think that you're a moron?

NUGENT: No one's ever *told* me that. [*laughter*] But I'm sure there's plenty out there who *do*. I'm *sure* of it.

☆☆☆

MORGAN: Do you always open up like this in all your interviews?

NUGENT: No, I don't. I was told that you were a big supporter of mine, and that you were *aware* of my career. That you weren't one of these fuckin' *defense mechanism* assholes that was looking for a *contest* in every statement I make. So I *have* opened up.

Quite honestly, my interviews do not come across in print. Most of the jive you read are fictional quotes. I don't know where they *fuckin'* get this stuff. I'm an intense individual and, like I said, I'm my own worst enemy 'cause *unless* you're sitting here *with* me…

I'm sure that you have *no question* about any of my statements tonight. I'm sure that I have made myself *perfectly clear*. But I also guarantee that if you attempt to quote me in print, *no one will have a clue*. I guaran-fuckin'-tee it. Because it's not black and white. What I'm saying *is* black and white. What I believe is what I believe. But in print, it loses…

MORGAN: The emotion?

NUGENT: Certainly. And certainly where I'm coming from. You know what I mean? It *ain't* gonna happen. The only way it'll happen is if someone does more of a commentary. It you try *quotin'* me, it'll come off… [*pauses*] It'll come off *funny*… [*laughs*] They're always *funny*. But the essence is *gone with the fuckin' wind*.

But I still conduct interviews because I genuinely enjoy interplay. And I genuinely enjoy communication; that's one of the reasons why I make music. And it's one of the reasons why I'm more than glad to voice my opinions and my commitments to you because I'm *proud* of them. I believe that they are well learned. And I believe that I am cognizant of situations and conditions in this world that I *have* formed opinions on. And I don't think I am *casual* about them, I think I'm very *sincere* about them. And I would like that that would be conveyed, 'cause I can enjoy it when someone is sincere.

When I read that someone makes a statement, and I believe in it, I *like* that person.

— **previously unpublished, 2021**
(complete unedited version, recorded on December 10th 1987)

JOHNNY WINTER

ANNABELLA LWIN

GARY NUMAN

JEFF BECK

**NEW
YORK
DOLLS**

**GRACE
SLICK**

**KIKI
DEE**

This is the West, sir. When a fictitious movie review gets reprinted as fact on a DVD, you don't need a cigarette smoking man to know which way the conspiracy blows.

"Mayor Of The Sunset Strip is the greatest rock n' roll movie ever made, and the first great rock movie of the 21st Century"
—Jeffrey Morgan, CREEM Magazine

"Wow! Great!,[1] Mayor Rules!,[2] A real-world version of 'Zelig',[3] The best movie about being a DJ since Howard Stern's 'Private Parts',[4] An excellent film,[5] Fascinating,[6]"

1. LA Daily News 2. San Francisco Chronicle 3. NY Daily News 4. Hits Magazine 5. Los Angeles Times 6. Rolling Stone

"Timeless,[1] Absorbing,[2] Improbably rich,[3] Wonderful,[4] Witty and deeply touching...Brilliant,[5] Rodney's story leaves you changed forever,[6]"

1. Salon.com 2. Chicago Tribune 3. NY Daily News 4. Chicago Sun-Times 5. Houston Chronicle 6. Ain't It Cool News

Rodney & Coldplay

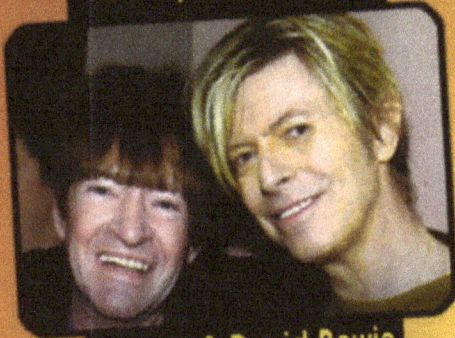

Rodney & David Bowie

BUST NO 1
RODNEY BINGENHEIMER
This Is Rodney Bingenheimer (Shout! Factory)

VARIOUS ARTISTS
Mayor Of The Sunset Strip (Shout! Factory)

FADE IN.
WEST HOLLYWOOD, CA.
4:17 AM

☆☆☆

ASSISTANT DIRECTOR SKINNER: What are we *doing* here, Agent Mulder?

SPECIAL AGENT DANA SCULLY: I was beginning to wonder that myself. Why *did* your contact insist on meeting us inside an abandoned record store? [*looking around with her flashlight*] I never thought downloading would put so many record stores out of business so quickly.

SPECIAL AGENT FOX MULDER: Supply and demand, Scully. When the supply chain artificially inflates prices, consumer demand will always migrate to a cheaper alternative.

SCULLY: [*surprised*] Mulder, I'm impressed!

MULDER: That's not me, Scully, that's according to the great economic philosopher Calvin. [*pauses*] Or was it Hobbes?

SCULLY: But why an empty record store?

MULDER: Because he fears retaliation by the Recording Industry Association Of America and knows that a record store is the *last* place they'd look for him in. Isn't it ironic?

SCULLY: Oh, I *love* that song!

SKINNER: Retaliation for *what*, Agent Mulder?

MULDER: For blowing the lid off the biggest audio conspiracy in the history of the human eardrum.

SCULLY: What are you saying, Mulder? That the federal government is allowing aliens to embed abduction homing frequencies in their CDs and DVDs as a new anti-piracy initiative? That *that's* the reason why so many record stores have gone out of business?

MULDER: That's *exactly* what I'm saying, Scully. Once the rumors began circulating, people realized that downloading was the only safe way to avoid the alien's identifying frequencies.

SCULLY: But Mulder, wouldn't it make more sense if the RIAA had the

frequencies embedded in the *downloaded* tracks? That way aliens would abduct the downloaders and not the honest consumer.

MULDER: That was the idea. But because the recording industry is dumber than a bag of rocks, they managed to get it backwards. Now the RIAA doesn't want it known that their law-abiding paying customers are the ones who are really at risk of being abducted. Talk about your *caveat emptor*.

SCULLY: Wait… Mulder, do you hear that?

MULDER: I don't hear anything. But then again, I haven't been able to hear properly ever since I skipped class to see Alien Sex Fiend open for Alice Cooper back in 1986.

SKINNER: No, I hear it too. It seems to be coming from that soundtrack section over there. Ye cats, what *is* that unearthly racket?

MULDER: [*listening*] Oddly enough, it's "School's Out" by Alice Cooper.

SCULLY: Mulder, someone's coming!

MULDER: That must be my contact.

SKINNER: I can see him now. It's…it's…

RODNEY BINGENHEIMER: Hi everybody!

SCULLY: Mulder, do you know who this is?

MULDER: Of course I do, Scully. This is my contact, 'Godhead.'

RODNEY: No, no, I'm—

SCULLY: It's Rodney Bingenheimer!

SKINNER: *Who?*

SCULLY: Rodney Bingenheimer of "Rodney's English Disco" and "Rodney On The ROQ" fame! I used to read about him every month in *Hit Parader*. Did you know that Frank Zappa wrote a song about him? So did Brian Wilson of The Beach Boys.

MULDER: I was always a *Circus Raves* man, myself.

SCULLY: Mulder, you couldn't *ask* for a better contact! He knows *everybody* personally.

SKINNER: Just exactly who *do* you know, Mr. Bingenheimer?

RODNEY: Oh, gee, I don't know. Just about everyone, I guess. The Beatles, Elvis Presley, The Mothers, Bob Dylan, The Runaways, Kim Fowley, The Rolling Stones, Jerry Vale, The Monkees, David Bowie, The Ramones, Led Zeppelin, The Doors, Alice Cooper, Binky, Elton John, Sonny & Cher, Nancy Sinatra—

SCULLY: You know The First Lady Of Rock? That is so cool! You know, I always considered "Boots" to be the world's first women's liberation anthem.

RODNEY: Oh yeah, most definitely. Nancy's Godhead!

MULDER: Nancy Sinatra's Godhead? I thought *you* were Godhead.

RODNEY: Oh, no, I'm just Rodney.

SKINNER: Agent Mulder says you have something for us.

RODNEY: Yes, I do! Here, I want you to have these limited edition promotional copies of my new single. It's a remix of a track that's on the new *Mayor Of The Sunset Strip* soundtrack album. And here's a copy of the full album.

SCULLY: I've seen that movie, Mulder. *Mayor Of The Sunset Strip* is a great documentary about Rodney. It's funny and heartwarming and everybody that Rodney knows is in it.

RODNEY: [*pulling a sheet of paper out of his pocket*] Here's a new review from CREEM, America's Only Rock 'n' Roll Magazine: "*Mayor Of The Sunset Strip* is the greatest rock 'n' roll movie ever made, and the first great rock movie of the 21st Century."

SCULLY: They're right, it is! Mulder, did you know that Rodney was in the audience of every American music television show ever made? In the movie you can see him on *The Ed Sullivan Show* and *Hollywood Palace* and *Shindig* and *Hullabaloo* and *American Bandstand* and *Soul Train* and *In Concert* and *The Midnight Special* and—

MULDER: *Saturday Night Live With Howard Cosell*?

RODNEY: [*thinking*] Not that one, no.

SKINNER: Is *this* why you brought us here, Mr. Bingenheimer? To give us these records?

RODNEY: Yes, it's a great soundtrack album! Alice is on it, as well as David Bowie, T. Rex, Ramones, Brian Wilson, The Byrds, Courtney Love's Hole, The Smiths, Blur, Asylum Choir, Dramarama with Chris Carter—

SCULLY: *Who?*

MULDER: Chris Carter, the greatest wide receiver of all time.

SKINNER: What makes you think we'd be interested in all this?

RODNEY: Because X is on the album as well. And since you run the X fan club, I thought you might want—

MULDER: We don't run the X fan club. We run the X-Files.

RODNEY: The X-Files?

SCULLY: A highly classified paranormal division of the FBI.

RODNEY: The FBI? Oh, okay. [*pauses*] Well, I guess you can still keep the two records. You know, if you save the promotional disc, in a few years you can probably sell it on eBay.

MULDER: That's not a bad idea. Thanks, I will.

VOICE: Police! Freeze!

MULDER: Hey, what *is* this? Who *are* you people?

SGT. JOE FRIDAY: My name's Friday. I'm a cop. I'm taking you in on a 714: unlawful entry into an abandoned record store with an intent to sell records which are clearly marked "Not For Sale - For Promotional Use Only."

SKINNER: You're making a big mistake.

We're FBI agents!

FRIDAY: You can tell it to the Captain, downtown.

SCULLY: What do you want from *us?*

FRIDAY: Just the facts, ma'am. Let's go. [*getting into a squad car*] Can we drop you off somewhere, Mr. Mayor?

RODNEY: Oh, no thanks. I think I'll stroll down to the Continental Hyatt and grab some breakfast.

FRIDAY: Well, thanks again for your assistance. We've been trying to catch this X gang red-handed for months.

RODNEY: [*waving as the squad car pulls away*] See you on the Strip!

ANNOUNCER: The record review you have just read is true. None of the names have been changed to protect the innocent. Although acquitted on the more serious charge of record piracy, Assistant Director Walter Skinner; Special Agent Fox Mulder; and Special Agent Dana Scully were all found guilty of overacting. They were sentenced to life in syndication. Despite overwhelming evidence to the contrary, Rodney Bingenheimer still insists that he is not Godhead. This has been a MARK VII production.

FADE OUT.

— **CREEM, May 2004**

DISSIPATED ENOUGH TO QUALIFY

THE
JEFFREY
MORGAN
STORY

by J. Mark Berkowitz

AN UNDERHANDED OVERVIEW

Fatefully born on the same day that "(We're Gonna) Rock Around The Clock" by Bill Haley & His Comets was released, Jeffrey Morgan is the authorized biographer of Alice Cooper, having written Alice's definitive biography "Alcohol and Razor Blades, Poison and Needles: The Glorious Wretched Excess of Alice Cooper, All-American" which appears in the critically acclaimed best selling 1999 Warner Bros. box set *The Life and Crimes of Alice Cooper*.

☆☆☆

In March 2003, the noted *International Journal Of Academic Psychiatry* cited Morgan's authorized biography in their paper "From Alice Cooper To Marilyn Manson: The Significance Of Adolescent Antiheroes." To say that Morgan got a lot of mileage out of *that* attribution would be an understatement.

In 2011, the Rock And Roll Hall Of Fame And Museum further cited Morgan's authorized biography as "Recommended Reading" in their official Alice Cooper inductee bio—an attribution that the Rock Hall later removed from their website after discovering how much mileage Morgan

was getting out of it. Fortunately, the original attributed webpage is still permanently available for viewing via the Internet Archive. You could look it up.

Morgan is also the authorized biographer of The Stooges, having co-written their definitive biography "The Stooges, Yes" which appears in Robert Matheu's best selling critically acclaimed 2009 Abrams hardcover book *The Stooges: The Authorized And Illustrated Story*, which Morgan additionally edited.

Rock criticism's most beloved satirist and the highly respected Don of American Rock Critics, Morgan became the *de facto* Canadian Editor of CREEM: America's Only Rock 'n' Roll Magazine after Lester Bangs personally invited him to write for the legendary music publication in 1974.

Morgan's poetry has been published in *Rolling Stone* magazine; and his award-winning newspaper column *Jeffrey Morgan's Media Blackout* appeared for over a decade in Detroit's *Metro Times* and on RocksBackpages.com.

☆☆☆

THE DC & MARVEL LETTERS

Morgan's writing career began at the tender age of 12 when DC Comics published his first work in the comic book letters section of *Batman* #182 (August

1966). He never wrote another letter to DC but several years later began writing numerous letters to the Marvel Comics Group. A number of these letters were printed during the early '70s in the letters section of such Marvel comics as *Fantastic Four* #95, *The Amazing Spider-Man* #82, *The Avengers* #73, *Sgt. Fury And His Howling Commandos* #78, and *Conan The Barbarian* #5. More often than not, whenever one of his letters wasn't published, he received a compensatory Marvel No-Prize in the mail.

It was during this second letter writing phase that Morgan's first known piece of satirical writing was published. In the letters section of *Captain America* #122 (February 1970), he had two consecutive letters printed: the first under his own name and address and, directly beneath it, a second separately-sent letter which he'd signed with the name of deceased villain Baron Zemo.

In it, "Zemo" implored Marvel writer/editor Stan "The Man" Lee against resurrecting Cap's former World War II teen partner Bucky Barnes in favor of himself: "I'm begging you, Stan—keep the kid dead and let me return!" Stan's reply: "Sooo! The infamous Baron Zemo is alive and well in Toronto, ehhh? (TORONTO?!?)"

Jeffrey Morgan Photo © Tom Robe

⋆⋆⋆

NATIONALLY LAMPOONED

Over the next few years, Morgan's style of Marvel Comics letter writing would become so pervasively distinctive that the iconoclastic American humor magazine *National Lampoon* parodied his letter writing style in their "Is Nothing Sacred?" issue (January 1972). In the Marvel pastiche "Son-O'-God Comics," which was co-written by Canadian associate editor Michel Choquette, the first letter in the fake letters section at the end of the story was attributed to having been written by "Stan Spooner, Toronto, Canada." This parody letter accurately spoofed Morgan's writing style in tone and spirit, right down to the prescient "Yours in Christ" closing salutation.

⋆⋆⋆

THE CREEM YEARS

By this time Morgan had ceased writing letters to Marvel, having turned his attention to a major music publication from Michigan that billed itself as CREEM: America's Only Rock 'n' Roll Magazine. In a recurrence of what had happened earlier at DC and Marvel, CREEM editor Lester Bangs began publishing Morgan's irreverent letters adding, as he did with every letter, a small comment after each one. At one point, when Morgan enquired as to whether the magazine had a Creemsters Union, Bangs editorially replied: "Yeah, you're dissipated enough to qualify?" Shortly thereafter, Morgan received an unsolicited letter from Bangs inviting him to write for the magazine.

Morgan's first official appearance in CREEM, however, wasn't as a writer but as a photographer. In the March 1975 issue Bangs printed a photo that Morgan had taken the previous year of Lou Reed and Alice Cooper singing "Goodnight Ladies" on stage at Massey Hall to illustrate "Let Us Now Praise Famous Death Dwarfs," his humorously combative cover story about Reed.

Later that October, Morgan's first published record review (of David Bowie's 1965 Pye single "Can't Help Thinking About Me") ran in CREEM, thus beginning what was to become a marathon run. He was the first writer to casually refer to the magazine in print simply as "America's Only," an abbreviated form of affection which is still used to this day—albeit only by Morgan.

⋆⋆⋆

THE PHOTOGRAPHIC ARCHIVE

As noted above, Morgan began his rock photography career in 1974. After spending fifteen years taking almost a thousand photographs, he did what anyone else would do with such an historical archive of previously unseen and unpublished images: Morgan put them at the bottom of a closet and promptly forgot all about them for close to half a century.

⋆⋆⋆

THE CPI YEARS

In 1975, founding Editor-In-Chief Marty "The Zog" Herzog hired Morgan to be the Editor of what was literally Canada's Only Rock 'n' Roll Magazine—a new monthly Canadian rock rag which would undergo three different successive name changes during its lifespan, from *Cheap Thrills* to *StageLife* to *Roxy*. Distributed free all across Canada from its inception to its untimely demise in 1978, the magazine was published by Concert Productions International, a company headed by future Rolling Stones concert promoter Michael Cohl.

It was during this time that CPI gave Morgan ongoing access to a pair of front row center seats at Maple Leaf Gardens, thus enabling him to photograph a plethora of arena acts that performed in Toronto, all in their youthful prime.

⋆⋆⋆

MACHINE ROCK

It was in April 1975, while writing for *Cheap Thrills*, that Morgan created his literary alter ego Machine Rock as a means by which he could adopt a far more strident stance in his writing than usual—which wasn't exactly milquetoast to begin with. When Tee Vee Records released a compilation record six months later called "Machine Rock" (TeeVee 1038), Cohl and his business partner Bill Ballard briefly considered suing for damages until they found out that Morgan hadn't registered his alias as a trademark. Eventually "The Machine" would go on to host his own local weekly cable television program and appear in CREEM whenever Morgan wanted to write about himself—which was often.

⋆⋆⋆

MARLENE DIETRICH

Little is known about Morgan's encounter with legendary actress and singer Miss Marlene Dietrich, other than the fact that it occurred on February 25, 1975 at the Royal York Hotel in Toronto. For it was on this date that Miss Dietrich personally addressed a large manila envelope to

Don't laugh. Twelve years later, my poetry was published in *Rolling Stone*.

Brown News and Views

Published by The Brown Home and School Association

VOLUME 20	NOVEMBER, 1965	NUMBER 2

FROM THE CHILDREN

The Sun

The sun comes on me day by day
Finding me in every way.
It shines on all my books and face
And dodging it, oh! what a race.

Jeffrey Morgan,
Grade 6, Room 4.

ELEVEN DAYS

The 22nd we got out
And once outside we all did shout.
For Christmas holidays now were here
And it was the season for good cheer.

But now the 3rd is here, alas,
And all those days have gone to pass.
So, to our desks we come once more,
Knowing there's lots of work in store.

Jeffrey Morgan, Rm. 4, Gr. 6.

Morgan, writing his name out in full on its front. Then she picked up the telephone in her suite and called him at home. The reason why she did this, as well as the envelope's contents, remains unknown.

☆☆☆

GLENN GOULD & THE CBS YEARS

At the same time that he was writing for CREEM and CPI, Morgan also served as the staff copywriter for CBS Records Canada. Late one afternoon in 1978, Morgan received a telephone call at home from iconoclastic pianist Glenn Gould, who had called to explain why he didn't want to be interviewed for an anniversary box set that Morgan was writing for CBS. Mr. Gould then stayed on the line for 40 minutes, during which time he assumed a number of vocal characterizations and discussed everything from Bach to Petula Clark.

A highlight of the conversation was when Morgan pointed out to Mr. Gould that rock music would always have the advantage over classical music in that, with classical music, the closest you could ever come to approximating what the original composer had in mind was by using an original transcription and period instruments. However, with rock music, you always had a definitive recorded version by the artist from which you could build on. After a moment's pause Mr. Gould replied: "You know, I never *thought* of that before!"

Morgan wrote his first set of liner notes while at CBS, for an album of baroque music by classical guitarist Liona Boyd. Encouraged by his earlier classical-rock conversation with Glenn Gould, Morgan purposefully and incongruously wrote the album notes in his distinctive CREEM rock critic style in a deliberate attempt to boost Miss Boyd's career and increase her record sales by introducing her music to a wider audience.

Unfortunately, the day before the final artwork was scheduled to go to the printers, Miss Boyd paid a surprise visit to the CBS art department and immediately ordered the liner notes removed after she'd read them, exclaiming: "You can't print that! He makes me sound like a rock star!" Fearing further reprisals, CBS promptly acquiesced and destroyed all copies of the artwork which contained Morgan's notes.

In light of his later highly-successful myth-building work with Alice Cooper and The Stooges, one can only wonder at how high Miss Boyd's star would have ascended, had she not… Well, he *tried* to help her.

Jeffrey Morgan Photo © Tom Robe

☆☆☆

THRILLING WOMEN

In 1975 Morgan met conceptual illustrator and graphic designer Dean Motter, with whom he would collaboration on a number of projects over the ensuing decades—not the least of which were published in *Cheap Thrills*, where Mr. Motter served as art director under the aforementioned Mr. Herzog's aegis.

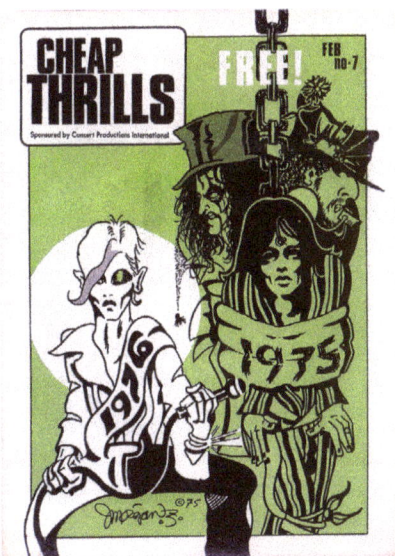

Between 1977 and 1980, Motter and Morgan recorded an "ambient electronic avant-garde progressive art rock album" titled *Thrilling Women* under the collective band name of the Air Pirates. The first recorded instance of a Canadian supergroup, the album features the work of over a dozen international musicians including vocalist Paul Robinson of The Diodes; guitarist Toby Swann of The Battered Wives; and saxophonist Andy

Haas of Martha & The Muffins.

In 2011, the exhaustively-titled *Thrilling Women: The Lost Air Pirates Sessions, Toronto, 1977-1980* was finally released by Bongo Beat Records as a digital download. *Thrilling Women* was given a physical release in 2020.

☆☆☆

MISTER X

It was during this time that Motter was also busy creating *Mister X*, the graphic novel for which he is best known and which he wrote between June 1984 and August 1988. When Motter left the first color series to work on other projects, he asked Morgan to assume the writing duties for a second black and white series which appeared from April 1989 to March 1990. In 2008, once again at Motter's behest, Morgan returned to Somnopolis and wrote the introduction to the first volume of Dark Horse Comics' hardcover omnibus *Mister X: The Archives*.

In 2011, Dark Horse Comics published Morgan's graphic novel *The Brides Of Mister X and Other Stories* in a deluxe hardcover edition. *Rolling Stone* called *The Brides Of Mister X* "one of the 50 best non-superhero graphic novels."

☆☆☆

STAR*REACH & STERANKO

Prior to this, Morgan's first comic book writing credit appeared in "the most important comic book of the 1970s" when he wrote "Murphy's Law," a 16 page cover story which appeared in *Star*Reach #16* (April 1979). Five years earlier, comics legend Jim Steranko had published one of Morgan's photographs in his magazine *Comics Scene*: a black and white portrait of *Conan* artist Barry Windsor-Smith.

☆☆☆
ALICE COOPER & THE STOOGES

Not bad for someone who's never stepped foot in Michigan.

☆☆☆
THE ROCK CRITIC HALL OF FAME

In 1975, Morgan founded the Rock Critic Hall Of Fame whose first, and only, inductees are: Al Aronowitz, Ralph J. Gleason, Lillian Roxon, Gloria Stavers, and Derek Taylor.

☆☆☆
ROCK CRITICS WITHOUT BORDERS

But of all these august accomplishments, Morgan is best known as the rock evangelist founder of the influential international humanitarian aid organization Rock Critics Without Borders. When he created RCWB, one of his primary goals was to spread the literal word of rock music around the world through the expert applied use of informed rock criticism.

For over a century, Morgan's missionaries have traversed the far-flung corners of the globe and converted millions of ignorant savages to this enlightened cause. Thanks to his pioneering work in this field, tens of thousands of government departments have been created over the past half century which do just that—and a whole lot more.

Some of these officially sanctioned RCWB affiliated agencies include: Plotzen Roll (Israel); Her Majesty's Official Ministry Of Popular Music (England); Heil Rockenplatz (Germany); Rockit Unit (USSR); Rock 'n' Roll Canada (People's Republic Of Canuckistan); and the Bureau Of Alcohol, Tobacco, Sex, Drugs, and Rock 'n' Roll (USA). Under Morgan's direct leadership, the research and development wings of these departments have been responsible for creating the most exciting innovations in the history of rock 'n' roll.

In the 1950s, in partnership with Tip Top Tailors, Morgan introduced the tradition of rock musicians wearing suits and ties on stage so wary parents would feel more at ease with this new form of entertainment. Then in the 1960s, he teamed up with Consolidated Edison to develop the powerful electrical infrastructure needed to provide terawatts of clean renewable energy to every major outdoor peace and love festival from Altamont to Medicine Ball Caravan. And in the 1970s, he joined forces with the elite scientists of Dow Chemical to invent the weapons-grade pyrotechnics which made the theatrical rock era possible.

As Morgan writes in his autobiography *Ich habe die leute gezwungen, alles über mich zu lesen GEGEN IHREN WILLEN!* (translated from the German):

"Rock Critics Without Borders has been there every decibel of the way and we're not finished yet. I've just signed a memo of understanding with Weyland-Yutani and the Union Aerospace Corporation to expand my ministry off world to other planets. If there's life on Mars, you can bet that I'll find it and convert it. The first one hundred years have been great, but I guarantee that the best has yet to come. You have my word on it because my name is Jeffrey Morgan—and I *am* rock 'n' roll."

☆☆☆

J. MARK BERKOWITZ *is a noted enviromusicologist and socio-sexual activist. His seminal article "The Hi-Fi Hipster" appeared in the March 1955 issue of* **Playboy** *and is recognized as being the first recorded instance of erudite rock criticism published anywhere in the world. He lives in Sweden with his wife, the award-winning adult movie actress Fårö Syrjäniemi.*

LINDA McCARTNEY

BRUCE
SPRINGSTEEN

J. GEILS BAND

CLARENCE
CLEMONS

LARRY FAST

GEORGE HARRISON

PHIL LYNOTT

AN AFTERWORD
AND A WARNING
by Alice Cooper

Don't believe a word of what you just read.

Well, okay, maybe a word here or there.
But Jeffrey can really write, no question about it.
Whether it's true or not, who knows.

Alice Cooper

ALICE COOPER *is rock 'n' roll's foremost legendary statesman of outrage.*

ARMED SERVICES EDITION

BOOKS ARE WEAPONS - in a free democracy everyone may read what he likes. This book is published by Editions For The Armed Services, Inc., a nonprofit organization established by the Council On Books In Wartime.

It is intended for exclusive distribution to members of the American Armed Forces and is not to be resold or made available to civilians. This edition is made available only until normal free publishing, interrupted by Axis aggression, can be reestablished.

After you have finished reading this book, why not give it to someone in the Armed Services who needs good reading?

Pass it on!

BOOKS ARE WEAPONS ★ ★ IN THE WAR OF IDEAS

A NOTE FROM THE PUBLISHER

❋

The publisher would like to take this opportunity to correct a number of items which appear as statements of fact in Jeffrey Morgan's *Rock Critic Confidential*.

A thorough investigation into the matter has concluded that the statements made by Mr. Morgan were, in fact, completely false and deliberately made to misinform the reader including, but not limited to, the obfuscating use of a fictional alias.

The publisher regrets the errors.

❋

CORRECTIONS

❋

Martha Raye is not the mother of Johnny Ray. Brian Jones was not pushed. Elvis is not Orion. Nothing happens if you watch *Pink Floyd At Pompeii* while listening to Judy Garland At Carnegie Hall. Alice Cooper did not play Eddie Haskell on *Leave It To Beaver.* Axl Rose is not a member of Falun Gong. Eugene Levy never sued John Lennon. Jerry Mathers was not killed in Vietnam and he is not the father of Eminem. Lou Christie does not make good cookies. Bob Dylan was not replaced by a double after dying in a motorcycle accident. The Beatles are not Klaatu. Ricky Nelson is not a member of Cheap Trick. The woman heard yelling "'Paint It Black,' you devils!" on *Get Yer Yas-Ya's Out!* is not Lynette "Squeaky" Fromme. Will Rogers never met Allan Klein. The New Vaudeville Band never released an album titled *Jesse Winchester's Cathedral.* Robert Johnson was not stood up at the crossroads. Clapton is not God. Paul is not dead. Jim isn't alive, man. Andy Warhol did not produce *Screaming Lord Sutch And Heavy Friends.* Lou Reed and Rex Reed are not twin brothers. Lester Bangs did not play Michael Stivic on *All In The Family.* Pete Townshend never took part in The Battle Of Britain. Paul Reubens did not replace Freddie Mercury in Queen. The Band did not record *Music From Pink Flamingoes.* John Bonham was not one of The Marx Brothers. Slade were not illiterate. Bryan Ferry never crossed the Mersey. Mick Jagger did not kill the Kennedys and neither did you. A splendid time isn't guaranteed for all.

And, in the end, the love you take isn't equal to the love you make.

❋

THANK YOU KINDLY
by JEFFREY MORGAN

"To exceed the limits of a formula without destroying it is the dream of every magazine writer who is not a hopeless hack."
— *Raymond Chandler*

☆☆☆

Thanks be to God, absolutely *none* of the words which appear in this autobiography would *ever* have been written had it not been for the selfless unsolicited intervention of Lester Bangs in the summer of 1974. I tell that story on page 144 of the HarperCollins hardcover *CREEM: America's Only Rock 'n' Roll Magazine*, so I won't reiterate it here.

What I will say, however, is that I'm eternally and deeply indebted to my parents, **Anne Morgan** and *Joe Morgan*, for a lifetime of unconditional love and lenience.

Whatever writing ability I may have is due in large part to my Father, who was the sports director at CKFH before becoming the news director at CKEY. Prior to that, he was the editor of *The Thoroughbred* magazine and, during the '50s, wrote a sports column "Let's Talk Sports With Joe Morgan" in *FLASH* weekly. For half a century, *FLASH* ("No Fear – No Favor – The People's Paper") reigned supreme as Toronto's most sensational and longest running crusading tabloid and scandal sheet.

Which, speaking of long running half century marks and sensational scandal sheets, brings us to *Rock Critic Confidential*.

☆☆☆

In his Introduction to the above-noted *CREEM: America's Only Rock 'n' Roll Magazine*, Professor Brian J. Bowe describes me as being "…CREEM's longest-serving and most inventive writer…" Given my record-setting twenty year tenure at CREEM (thirteen years writing for the magazine in one hundred and fifty-eight consecutive issues, plus an additional seven years writing for the original CREEM website), I can live with that on both counts—especially the *inventive* part because at

---

Page Twenty-two   **FLASH**   **MARCH 27, 1954**

Let's talk Sports *with Joe Morgan*

HORSE RADISH: How good is Cain Hoy Stable's Turn-To? Where does the imported Irish-bred colt rank in the overall sophomore picture? What are his chances in the Kentucky Derby, Preakness and Belmont Stakes? These are the questions we hope to answer before the first of these classic races comes up for decision the first week in May.

Quite frankly this observer was not greatly impressed by Turn-To's comparatively easy Flamingo Stakes victory. The same hard, sunbaked, speed-conducive strip prevailed for that race as it did for all the other stakes of the Hialeah meeting. Speedhorses or sprint-types were successful in almost all the stakes races on Hialeah's main course this winter. Most of these winners lacked the class or staying ability at the northern courses during the 1953 season.

TURN-TO

Unquestionably Turn-To is a top-notch speedster or sprinter. But will he carry this speed an appreciable distance over the sandy Long Island ovals or the normally deep and tiring Keenland and Churchill Downs courses? The pace will be a sizzler in the sophomore races to come. The Guggenheim colorbearer will be making or forcing the pace throughout. Porterhouse, Determine, Double Speed, Duc de Fer, Swift Sword, Artismo, Best Years, Hasty Road, Errard King, By Jeepers and many others are in the speed horse category. Many will fall by the wayside but not without a shot at the "gold and glory." Any combination of three will make for a sustained pace against Turn-To and enhance the chances of a come-from behinder. Goyamo, Fisherman and Correlation appear the best of this type.

Goyamo, fourth in the Flamingo after moving up boldly around the turn, is our future book pick for the Kentucky Derby. We like him because he performed well over a track that was definitely against him. This is a rugged colt handled by a top conditioner, Woody Stephens of Blue Man fame. The Royce Martin campaigner has slightly tender feet which caused him to pull up very sore almost lame, in all his appearances at Hialeah. The wonder is that he was able to win twice over the strip. He has been entered for the Florida Derby and will point for the race unless the Gulfstream track becomes too hard. Unfortunately, Turn-To was not nominated for this race and another meeting between this pair is unlikely before the Kentucky racing season.

America's Only I excelled at exceeding the limits of the rock criticism formula without destroying it; at least not *too* much.

Regardless of whether my words assumed the form of a television satire; multiple choice questionnaire; Rorschach ink blot test; or a John Lennon missing in action record review which radically contained no words whatsoever, CREEM *understood*. No other rock magazine, either then or now, ever had the supreme confidence to offer a writer such unprecedented creative latitude.

Not that my post-CREEM career has been any less inspired. Indeed, hardly a day goes by that I don't shake my head in bemused wonder at how the same Toronto high school teenager who bought multiple copies of *Killer* and *Raw Power* to repeatedly replace his worn out vinyl versions could somehow end up being the authorized biographer of both Alice Cooper *and* Iggy Pop & The Stooges. *Soli Deo gloria!*

☆☆☆

Regrets? I've had a few; most notably that I didn't have the opportunity to tape record the 40 minute telephone conversation I had with Glenn Gould when he unexpectedly called me at home in 1978. Likewise when Marlene Dietrich phoned in 1975.

Offsetting those omissions is the earlier occasion in 1962 when I had the opportunity to meet and shake hands with Moe Howard, Larry Fine, and Curly Joe DeRita at the *CNE Grandstand Matinee Fun-Fest*—a mandatory pre-requisite for any up-and-coming Stooges biographer.

And although I may have vexed a few folks along the way—both the CREEM and *Cheap Thrills* letters sections provide ample good-natured evidence of that—hopefully I've been able to amuse them as well.

Come rain or come shine, the following starting lineup of heavy hitters is hereby formally cited first and foremost for initially offering me the opportunity to elsewhere write the words in this book:

**LESTER BANGS
MARTIN W. HERZOG
ROBERT MATHEU**

Batting cleanup is the following phalanx of topnotch All Stars who came off the bench to provide assistance, encouragement, and advice far above and beyond the call of duty. Whether it be intentionally or inadvertently—either in person, on the telephone, or in writing—without them, I wouldn't constantly be looking around and asking myself that musical question: Well, how did I *get* here?

**Billy Altman
Alice Cooper
Dave DiMartino
Toby Mamis
Dean Motter
Brian Nelson
Richard Riegel
Tom Robe
Jaan Uhelszki**

Plus an additional clubhouse tip of the managerial cap to:

• **J. J. Kramer**, for his continued support and for generously allowing me to reprint my CREEM Magazine writing in *Rock Critic Confidential*. Without J. J.'s parents, Barry Kramer and Connie Kramer, there would have been no CREEM for me to write for back then—and without J. J. himself there would be no CREEM for you to enjoy today.

• **Sheryl Matheu**, for her ongoing assistance and for graciously allowing me to use the photographs of her late husband, *photographer extraordinaire* Robert Matheu. More than anyone else, Sheryl knows what *Rock Critic Confidential* meant to Robert and how pleased he would be to see it published with his work so prominently displayed, both on the front and back covers and within its pages.

• **Teddie Dahlin**, the visionary founder and CEO of New Haven Publishing. Collections of writing are a hard sell at the best of times and that goes triple for an autobiographical compendium of rock criticism—especially one which admirably ups the ante and regenerates the genre by being the first book by a rock critic published in a copiously illuminated paradigm-defining hardcover coffee table edition. If there's a safe haven for rock critics, it's New Haven.

• **Pete Cunliffe** of New Haven Publishing, for designing a book that sets new *nonpareil* standards of excellence against which all other rock writing books will forever be gauged. That's not hyperbole, that's a fact because it ain't bragging if you can back it up.

• **Ralph Alfonso, Pat Harbron, Tom Robe, John Rowlands, Carol Starr,** and **Paul Till** for selflessly contributing their photographs to *Rock Critic Confidential*. Having admired the images of these peerless professionals for decades, I'm extremely honored to have their stellar work appear in this book.

• **Harvey Hart**, noted award-winning film and television director (*Alfred Hitchcock, Star Trek, Columbo*), for advising me that I would need a longer lens on my Pentax if I was going to photograph rock concerts—and then coming to my aid by loaning me his own Canon camera and telephoto lens until I was able to buy a 135mm Zoomar for myself.

• **Wendy James**, perennial pen pal and my favorite swank back door cover girl. If anyone understands what the men don't know, it's this Rock 'n' Roll Queen, you know what I mean—long may she reign supreme.

☆☆☆

Finally, my sincere and utmost thanks to *you.*

Yours in Christ,

Jeffrey Morgan

Jeffrey Morgan
• New York • London • Paris
• Munich • Toronto

☆☆☆

Jeffrey Morgan's signature calligraphy by:

Miss Marlene Dietrich,
Royal York Hotel,
Toronto, February 25th 1975

AND IF THAT AIN'T ENOUGH TO MAKE YOU FLIP YOUR LID, THERE'S ONE MORE THING...

America's Only Rock 'n' Roll Magazine

CREEM

P.O. Box P-1064, Birmingham, Michigan 48012

Isn't it fun getting a rejection slip?

There are all kinds, you know. Most of us here at CREEM have been hit with just about every genre of rejection slip in the course of our lives, enabling us to study the subject in the most empirical fashion.

First, there is the businesslike, or standard form rejection slip: "Thank you for submitting the enclosed manuscript. Unfortunately, it is not at this time suitable for our needs. Please keep us in mind in the future."

Then there is the apologetic riff, common to many *Greening of America* type publications: "Please excuse this impersonal form of reply, but. . ." followed by the exact same words as the strictly-business number.

Sometimes, there is even the envelope you wrote your name and address on and affixed that stamp to originally, making you a bit queasy when you discover that there is absolutely nothing inside it but your manuscript, folded neatly and returned without a word of recognition.

Having studied the subject and put in field experience for as long as we have, we at CREEM know there is no "nice" way, no easy way to say No. So we won't. We will take this impossibly circuitous way to say thank you, and ask you to please try us next time.

Brian Wilson
Photo © Robert Matheu

If you're going to be an interesting critic,
you've *got* to have a little zing.

It's all right to be wrong,
but you've *got* to be interesting.

We're all in the same business.
We're entertaining the public.

Orson Welles

Thanks to you.

Jeffrey Morgan

Toronto, April 2021

www.ingramcontent.com/pod-product-compliance
Lightning Source LLC
Chambersburg PA
CBHW062009150426
42812CB00013BA/2581